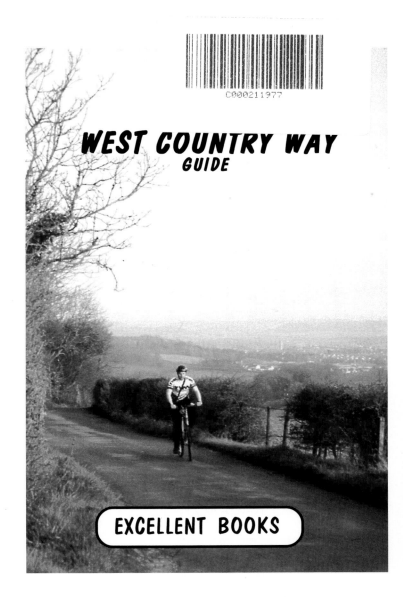

WEST COUNTRY WAY
GUIDE

EXCELLENT BOOKS

EXCELLENT BOOKS
94 BRADFORD ROAD
WAKEFIELD
WEST YORKSHIRE WF1 2AE
TEL / FAX: (01924) 315147

First Published 1998

ISBN 1 901464 03 2

Whilst the author has cycled and researched the route for the purposes of this
guide, no responsibility can be accepted for any unforeseen circumstances
encountered whilst following it. The publisher would, however, welcome any
information regarding any material changes and any problems encountered.

Front cover photo: Anstey Common, Exmoor
Rear cover photo: A quiet road near Glastonbury

Printed in Great Britain by
FM Repro Ltd.
Repro House, 69 Lumb Lane
Roberttown
Liversedge
West Yorkshire WF15 7NB

CONTENTS

A quiet minor road on rugged Exmoor (section 5)

INTRODUCTION

WHAT IS THE WEST COUNTRY WAY?

The answer is simply one of the best ways to see the varied and beautiful scenery of the south-west. Opened in May 1997, the 250 mile cycling route starts in the picturesque port of Padstow with a choice of finish in the once prestigious port city of Bristol or the refined architecture of modern day tourist mecca Bath. In between is a fantastic variety of countryside and settlements.

The brainchild of path- building charity Sustrans , the West Country Way is part of their strategy, implemented in conjunction with local authorities, for a National Cycle Network. The West Country Way is therefore an exciting leisure route in its own right but is also part of a national 'alternative' transport policy. In its final form it will link to routes in South Wales, extending to Land's End and along the bottom of the south-west peninsula.

It is intended for all levels and types of cyclist, though the emphasis is on tempting out those put off cycling by roads crowded with tons of speeding metal; ahead of them on the West Country Way lie miles of well-maintained, suitable off- road paths and quiet minor roads (occasional rougher sections such as the Grand Western Canal will be upgraded). Still at an interim stage of development, the route is constantly being improved and made safer for cycling by Sustrans. A good example is the new traffic-free section approaching Glastonbury from Bridgwater which now avoids a short but busy section of road alongside the River Brue.

Rather than follow a straight line from Padstow to Bristol / Bath the route follows several loops heading generally north-east. This slightly circuitous line of the route allows use of the best off-road paths along the way as well as travelling through beautiful and interesting places, such as the National Trust property of Knightshayes, and crucially it links with several train stations (hence the big loop south to Tiverton). It is designed for leisure riders to experience the changing character of the area as well as for those wanting to make local journeys by bike in a safe and practical manner.

WHAT TO EXPECT

Less experienced cyclists will find the route an exciting challenge whilst old hands will appreciate the effort and time-saving aspect of having a 'ready-made' route mapped out and well signed. The division of this guide into 'day' sections ranging from 21 to 36 miles is aimed at the less experienced; those well used to cycle touring will no doubt aim for 50 miles and up in a day.

SUSTRANS - THE CYCLE PATH CHARITY

Sustrans is short for sustainable transport and it is through the construction of a 6,500 mile National Cycle Network that this organisation hopes to promote this aim. Since its founding in 1980 Sustrans has seen a spectacular growth in popularity. The West Country Way is simply one part in the creation of a such a network. Over £40 million of Millennium funds have been earmarked to help in the construction of this cycle network. Sustrans aim to promote local journeys by bike and 'green tourism' as in the case of the West Country Way; for example it is estimated the Camel Trail (part of the West Country Way) alone generates £5.8 million a year. Sustrans also relies on income from members. For further details of Sustrans services contact:

SUSTRANS HEAD OFFICE
35 King Street, Bristol BS1 4DZ
(0117) 929 0888

The changing geography and surfaces under wheel make for a very varied route in terms of physical effort. The largely flat Camel and Tarka trails along with well-surfaced canal towpath sections are suitable for any level of rider. At the other end of the scale three major extended climbs (to Bodmin Moor, Exmoor and the Mendips) require good stamina which will be rewarded by magnificent views and long, speedy descents. Between these two lie a huge variety of surface and gradient; a specific idea of what to expect is given in the chapter descriptions. The only exception is a lack of steep, muddy, rocky off-road tracks favoured by hard-core mountain bikers. Starting in Padstow and heading generally north-east is strongly recommended as you will most probably be able to take advantage of the prevailing winds. They should be at your back, helping to push you along. Cycling into a wind can easily double or triple the effort involved and have a big effect on the time you take.

THE COUNTIES

CORNWALL

Often described as one of the most distinctive and characterful of English counties, probably due to several factors. Its Celtic heritage, distinctive landscape and climate and its relative underdevelopment compared to much of the rest of England have all played a part in creating this unique identity.

The Celtic people here (most closely related to the Bretons of western France) had their own **language** until the eighteenth century when it fell out of use; its influence lingers in many Cornish settlement names. The Celtic prefixes of Tre, Pen and Pol are oft-quoted examples meaning 'homestead', 'pool' and 'headland' respectively. The language survives today largely as a subject of academic study only.

The rugged and often beautifully barren nature of the **landscape** is also distinctively Cornish. 150 miles of Cornish coastline make it the longest of any county and its contrasts are glimpsed approaching Bude on the West Country Way; within a few miles of each other you can experience the fantastic contortions of the steep cliff strata at Millook and the wonderful golden beaches around Bude. Inland the granite mass of Bodmin Moor dominates the surrounding countryside. Treeless, like much of the rest of the county, its sides, often boulder-strewn, rise to summits of granite tors and Bronze Age remains are found in numerous places. Bodmin Moor also claims the county's highest point in Brown Willy (1375 ft). The relatively hard granite of Bodmin continues east and west to form the 'backbone' of Cornwall. At the coast the granite upland runs out to often steep cliffs and dramatic estuaries such as the Camel. These estuaries also house the majority of what few trees there are in the county.

Cornwall's **climate** is much influenced by its position as the 'boot' of England, jutting into the Atlantic between the Bristol and English Channels. Wet and warm compared to much of the rest of England, Cornwall's weather is very much influenced by its maritime position. Prevailing winds from the west should help to push you along the route although the northern coast often bears the brunt of the worst weather coming off the sea. Damp, mild conditions promote the growth of exotic looking plants you may see along the way.

The county has also had a turbulent and interesting **history**. Religious passions have always run strong here; 10,000 Cornishmen took part in the 1549 Prayer Book rebellion against the removal of Latin and Cornish from church services. The seventeenth century saw this conservative area stay fiercely loyal to the King in the Civil War; Charles II's letter of thanks for Cornwall's support still hangs in many churches. In the eighteenth century Methodism, with its stress on pious and charitable conduct, took deep root in the mining and farming communities. The coast has also influenced Cornwall's history; 'wreckers', contrary to their name, often did no more than take goods from wrecked ships and there is little evidence for widespread luring of ships onto rocks. Miners were often the worst culprits and if alcohol was on board scenes of mayhem would often ensue.

Traditional industries of **tin and copper mining** have declined to the point of extinction (1998 saw the closing of South Crofty, the last Cornish tin mine). Previously Cornish mines produced 50% of world tin and 75% of world copper. However, clay is still extracted on a significant scale; note Stannon clay workings passed on Bodmin Moor. **Fishing** has also declined considerably with lively fishing harbours such as Padstow the exception rather than the rule. **Farming**, especially dairying, continues and the county is famed for clotted cream. A hard-to-find traditional speciality is star-gazey pie, so called because the pilchards baked inside are left with the heads sticking through the crust. Of course the county's most enduring culinary legacy has been the Cornish pasty! **Tourism** is the most recent industry and a mainstay of the economy in many places; cycling the West Country Way you are contributing in sustainable fashion to this industry.

DEVON

Although the name of Devon is derived from the Celtic meaning 'people of the earth' it lacks the strong independent Celtic tradition of Cornwall, despite many other similarities. The West Country Way avoids the county's main upland mass, **Dartmoor**, which lies firmly in the south. Dartmoor, however, is the source of many of the county's rivers and is larger and higher than Bodmin Moor. The Torridge is joined by the Okement which rises on Dartmoor, as does the Taw. **Exmoor** (mainly in Somerset) appears less bleak, although it is still often windswept and unforgiving in bad weather. Much of the water from Exmoor runs into the River Exe, passing through Tiverton before going onto Exeter and the English Channel. In contrast to much of Cornwall a lot of the Devon countryside takes on a green, rolling aspect; this is especially noticeable approaching Black Torrington as you pass through numerous small, lush valleys inhabited by lively streams.

Devon's **climate**, like Cornwall's, has a marked north-south difference. Still generally mild and wet away from the uplands the southern coast is markedly milder and is known as the 'English Riviera'. Again, the north suffers stronger winds in autumn and winter and more sea mists in spring and summer.

The county has a strong **maritime history**. Much of this took place along the south coast but today only Plymouth remains as a major port. Devon is still associated, though, with great Elizabethan seafarers such as Drake, Raleigh, Hawkins and Grenville. The relatively empty quaysides of Bideford and Barnstaple, once important maritime centres, epitomise the decline of this tradition. The legacy of religion is seen mainly in an abundance of very similar rather plain-looking parish churches often worth a look inside for their intricate wood carving.

In terms of **industry** money from wool, important in medieval times, has left a great architectural legacy in places such as Tiverton. Dairying and Devon cream are well-known. Pottery and glass-making (the latter at Great Torrington) have stood the test of time well. As in Cornwall, the mining industry, particularly around Dartmoor, is now simply part of our industrial heritage. **Tourism** is now the principal industry.

A final feature of note is the profusion of quiet, winding country lanes in Devon, linking bartons (main farmsteads); its 8,000 mile road network is the longest of any English county. This spider's web of country lanes is especially good news for cyclists wanting to get away from busy traffic. Many are bordered by thickets of willow, alder and bramble which house abundant wildlife and are dotted with primroses in early spring.

SOMERSET

Geographically speaking Somerset shows perhaps the most variety within the smallest area of all the counties crossed. It takes the form of a plain, the Somerset Levels, covered in several places in a thick blanket of peat, and surrounded by several varied upland ranges. To the north-west Exmoor merges into the Brendon Hills and the Quantocks, whilst in the south-west the Blackdown Hills rise up and leave the Vale of Taunton Deane between the two. In the north-east the Mendips form a natural barrier in front of Bristol and Bath and in the south-east the Dorset Downs complete the encircling hills. Each range has its own distinct character, from the gorges and caves of the limestone Mendips to the rolling moors of Exmoor. In the centre of the Levels, no more than a ripple in their smooth surface, rise the gentle, green Polden Hills.

Mythology, violent protest and trade have all played a strong role in Somerset's **history**. It was part of the Celtic kingdom of Dumnonia along with Devon. The legend of King Arthur dates from this period and is shared with Cornwall. Arthur supposedly fought his last battle at Slaughterbridge near Camelford in Cornwall and was supposedly buried at Glastonbury in Somerset, also an early Christian centre and a place surrounded by several myths. The Monmouth Rebellion of 1685 was an attempt to unseat Charles II that attracted the support of several thousand peasants. It ended in complete failure at the battle of Sedgemoor and resulted in the death of Monmouth and many of his followers.

The **industrial revolution** ignored much of the south-west; canals were not built in sufficient quantity and the wool industry chose to develop on a large scale in Yorkshire rather than Somerset where it had put down initial roots (at Taunton and Wellington for example). A glance at a waterways map of England will show how poorly served the south-west was, with only Bude, the Grand Western and the Bridgwater and Taunton canals now partly remaining. Small scale industry did flourish; the manufacture of bricks and tiles using mud from the tidal River Parrett is detailed in the Somerset Brick and Tile Museum at Bridgwater. Cider is the most famed agricultural product and the locally produced brew can be bought throughout the county, although dairying and market gardening are also important. Of course **tourism** is also now a mainstay of the economy. Turning from work to leisure, look out for a number of skittle alleys along the way, often attached to pubs.

8

GETTING THERE AND AWAY

Arrive by train! This is the message Sustrans are trying to get across and rightly so. This has been made even easier due to the fact that one of the main regional railway companies in the south-west, Great Western, has introduced cheaper bike reservation fees on its services along with bike storage racks. However, privatisation has inevitably complicated the situation as another company, South Wales and West Railway, also runs services along much of the same track. This highlights the main problems of taking bikes on trains. Space is often limited on main lines where bikes are put in separate coaches and on branch lines you must simply wait and see if there is space in one of the normal carriages (usually at the back of the train). Privatisation has also lead to divergence in rules about carrying bikes on trains; some carriers may make a great effort to accommodate you whilst others might have unhelpful restrictions. The best rules are to **book ahead as early as possible** on main line journeys and on branch lines get to the guard as quickly as possible and be nice to him / her! A summary of the present situation in the West Country follows but you should always check up-to-date arrangements.

• On Inter-City journeys from the rest of the UK to Bristol bike reservations are necessary and generally cost £3. Again check details of your particular journey.
• On mainline journeys in the south-west (e.g Bristol - Taunton) reserving a bike place is necessary and will cost you £1 if booked at least two hours in advance (or the day before for early morning trains), one-way. Non-reserved spaces cost £3 one way or £6 return.
• If your journey is with South Wales and West Railway only two bikes will be allowed per train on main lines (£1 advance booking fee) and on branch lines they are taken free subject to availability. At the time of writing South Wales and West were not carrying bikes on the Bristol - Paignton line at all between 7.15 and 8.45 and 16.00 and 18.00.
• To check which operator you are travelling with in the West Country get hold of the Great Britain Passenger Railway Timetable. For all rail information contact **0345 484950**. If they are unable to help you they should put you in touch with the relevant rail company.
• There is no direct service to Padstow. Sustrans advise you to get off at **Bodmin Parkway** and go via the link route and the Camel Trail to Padstow (see map on page 10). There is direct access to the route at Barnstaple, Tiverton Parkway, Taunton and Bridgwater stations and the route finishes near both Bristol and Bath stations.

PREPARATION

The vast majority of 'West Country Wayers' are holidaying and usually take up to 10 days. Some keen cyclists, especially those with previous experience of the route, complete it much more quickly. This guide is split into 9 'day' sections, ranging from 20.5 to 36 miles, aimed at novice cyclists or those with plenty of time who want to take in some of the attractions. Section start and finish points are as near as possible to centres of population where accommodation is plentiful, but this is not always possible, especially on long sections over largely barren terrain such as Exmoor. It is still advisable to book accommodation as far in advance as practicable; this is especially the case if you are completing the route in summer or you are planning to stay in smaller settlements with only limited accommodation. Those wanting to camp along the way should certainly have some previous cycling experience and allow extra time as the extra equipment weight slows down even the fittest cyclist quite noticeably.

One of the most important factors in preparation is to have a realistic idea of what daily mileage you are comfortable in achieving; remember the West Country Way has a large range of terrain and difficulty, from the considerable challenge of Exmoor and the Mendips to flat cycle paths, so adjust time estimates accordingly. The route description profile and summary at the beginning of each section give a good idea of what to expect.

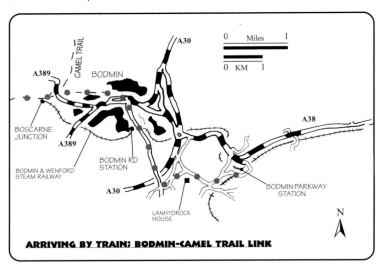

ARRIVING BY TRAIN: BODMIN-CAMEL TRAIL LINK

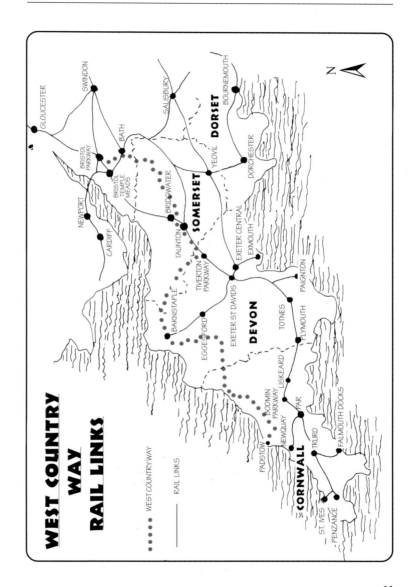

CHECKLIST   Basic essentials - there is a huge range of specialist cycling gear available. The list assumes you are staying B&B.

Clothing (winter / summer options included)
Helmet
High wicking inner layer (doesn't soak up sweat)
Cycle shirt and / or fleece top
Waterproof outer (preferably breathable-
well known makes are Goretex and Ceplex)
Gloves
Padded shorts
Thermal leggings
Tracksuit bottoms
Waterproof trousers
Boots / trainers / cycling shoes
At the least one change of clothing based
on the above
Sun hat / glasses / block

Tool Kit ('Multi-tools' may include several of these)
Small screwdriver
Small adjustable spanner
Allen keys (4,5,6 mm at least)
Pump
Spare brake blocks
Strong tape for quick repairs
Small container of chain and gear lubricant
Chain link extractor
Puncture kit & new inner tube

Other Essentials
Guide and maps (see map section)
Water bottle
Telephone contact of friends/family for
emergency
Toilet paper
Survival bag (used to keep warm if
stuck in foul weather conditions)

Bike lights
Money
Washing kit
Towel
Small first aid kit
Prescribed medication

This list will have obvious additions depending on the person; you may be camping or you may be enough of a mechanic to be able to replace a variety of parts.

MAINTENANCE

If you set off with a well-maintained bike the chances are that you won't need any of the tools or spares you take. A bike in good condition is especially important for such a long distance route. The most basic check should include the following list and if in any doubt about the state of your bike get it checked over properly at a good bike shop.

Important safety checks - do not neglect them!

Brake check - you should only be able to squeeze in front and rear brake levers a centimetre or two and braking response should be nice and sharp. However check brake blocks aren't rubbing on wheel rims, or even worse, tyres.

Brake cables - check that front and rear brake cables are not fraying. If they are replace them immediately.

Brake blocks - check that when you brake the blocks hit only the wheel rim, not the tyre and that there is plenty of wear left in the block.

Tyres - should be inflated to manufacturer's recommended pressure (as a rough guide you should just be able to depress the tyre when squeezing it). Check there is adequate tread.

Make sure the following are **lubricated**: front and rear brake pivots, moving parts of front and rear gear mechanisms, chain, brake lever pivots, entry and exit points of all cables. Keep these points well-lubricated during the ride.

Appropriate **screws and bolts** should be tight and you should check all gears are shifting properly.

For a full guide to buying and maintaining a bike see Haynes 'The Bike Book'.

CARRYING LOADS

Panniers are the ideal way to carry your extra gear. Small amounts of gear can be put in bum bags and the smaller seat and frame bags that fit around the bike or in handlebar bags or even a very small backpack. However, unless travelling very light in summer you will probably need panniers. Start off with rear panniers which sit on a frame over the rear wheel. Large amounts of extra gear will go in 'low rider' front panniers either side of the front forks. At all costs don't overload handlebar bags or a backpack - this will dangerously affect handling and balance.

Good preparation means a relaxing trip; resting outside Bishop's Palace, Wells (section 8)

13

SIGNING AND STAMPING POINTS

Many difficult junctions on the West Country Way have been waymarked by Sustrans. Direction signs should have a white number three on a red background, next to a white bike on blue background (shown on the front cover). If you are stuck at a junction check on road signs, gates and other nearby objects carefully. Also be aware that occasionally some of the signs may have been stolen or may have been twisted or otherwise vandalised, so you should also know where you are on any maps you are using. The red direction tips on the guide's maps have been written to highlight any potentially confusing junctions and any places where signs were missing at the time of writing the guide.

A Route Postcard is available from Sustrans which you can get stamped at various points along the route - also shown on the Sustrans map.

USING THIS GUIDE AND OTHER MAPS

Although you should be able to complete the West Country Way with an up to date edition of this book you are very strongly advised to take other maps. You should at the very least also take the Sustrans West Country Way map and use it in conjunction with this guide. Amongst many other features this map shows places where you can collect Sustrans ink stamps on a card. Ordnance Survey 1:50,000 Landranger maps show even more detail but you will need 7 of these to cover most of the route, which will work out at about £35 and a sizeable chunk of valuable storage space. You will also have to highlight the route on the OS maps. The maps you will need are as follows, but are only really feasible for use by a large group who can share the carrying space: Numbers 200 (Newquay & Bodmin), 190 (Bude & Clovelly), 180 (Barnstaple & Ilfracombe), 181 (Minehead & Brendon Hills), 193 (Taunton & Lyme Regis), 182 (Weston-super-Mare & Bridgwater) and 172 (Bristol & Bath).

Route maps in this book run consecutively, from west to east, so you should be able to follow the route just by turning the pages, without orientation problems. Simply hold the book normally, as you would when reading it, and route maps should be facing north. Some of the town maps have a different orientation but all feature a north indicator.

MAP KEY

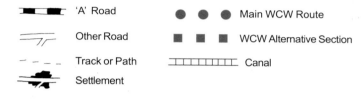

■■■	'A' Road
	Other Road
– – –	Track or Path
	Settlement

 River

B&B / CAMPSITE KEY

Information is based on individual questionnaires from owners; please confirm the information whilst booking. Other accommodation providers are listed with briefer details where they have not returned questionnaires. Brief details are also given of camping sites indicated by a ⚠ sign in the text.

B&B Abbreviations - prices are per person per night based on a double room.

£ = Under £10   ££ = Under £15   £££ = Under £20   ££££ = Under £25
£££££ = Over £25   PL = Packed Lunches (other meals also detailed)   DR = Drying Facilities   LAU = Laundry Facilities   SEC = Secure Bike Place   WKSH = Workshop facilities. The distance of the establishment from the route is given lastly, if known.

TRAILS USED BY THE WEST COUNTRY WAY

TRAIL NAME	*DETAILS*
Camel Trail	17 miles (27km) from Padstow to Merry Meeting, source of the Camel. Follows route of Bodmin - Padstow rail line. 350,000 visitors per year.
Tarka Trail	23 miles (37km). Petrockstow to Barnstaple. Based on a former railway line.
Bristol - Bath Railway Path	12.5 miles along the trackbed of the former Midland Railway.

1 PADSTOW - CAMELFORD

Section Distance 26 miles / 42 km   **Off-road** 16 miles / 26 km

The Route The flat and easy Camel Trail gives great views over the Camel Estuary, playground for yachtsmen, anglers, and waterskiers. After Wadebridge the easy trail continues through beautiful woodland before a tough climb to Bodmin Moor. Here the route levels out and follows twisting roads where careful navigation is required as the route isn't currently signed. The eerie scenery of the moor is breathtaking. If you want to explore Bodmin town or stay there it is an easy 1.5 miles off the main route on a spur.

PADSTOW - HISTORY AND ATTRACTIONS

• **Harbour town** tumbling attractively down the west bank of the Camel Estuary. Pleasure cruise runs from harbour as does regular passenger and cycle ferry to Rock. Active fishing industry (including crab, lobster and crayfish) supplies many local restaurants, including Rick Stein's premier seafood restaurant on Riverside.
• Strong **maritime tradition** including associations with Raleigh, Hawkins and Frobisher.
• **Prideaux Place** Elizabethan home of the Prideaux-Brune family. Extensive grounds, deer park and tea room. Views over Camel Estuary. Easter Sunday - 1st Oct. 1.30 - 5.00 (01841) 532411
• Unusual May Day **'Obby 'Oss** celebration. Uniquely costumed demonic figure parades through town, heading a procession. Possible pagan origin.
• **Parish Church of St. Petroc.** 15th century. Beautiful 'wagon' roof in south aisle. Open daily. St. Petroc, Cornwall's chief saint, arrived here in the 6th century and founded a monastery. Font of local blue-black Catacleuse stone.
• **Padstow Museum** Shows the history of the fishing port including 'Obby 'Oss information. Easter - Sept. Small admission charge.
• **Padstow Shipwreck Museum** Relics from local wrecks and display. South Quay. April 1st - Oct 31st. Lobster storage tanks next to the museum can be viewed for a small charge.
• **Metropole Hotel** Built in the late 19th century, when Padstow was then end of a major rail line from Waterloo, it adds an air of grandeur to the town.
• **Abbey House** on North Quay is one of the oldest buildings in Padstow.
• Other historic buildings include the **Almshouses** on Middle Street and fine houses on Church St. that belonged to sea captains and merchants.
• Memorials to **Claude Berry** and **Stephen Fuller** (writers born in Padstow) are near the north quay with fine views over the estuary which houses **Doom Bar**, responsible for wrecking many ships.

16

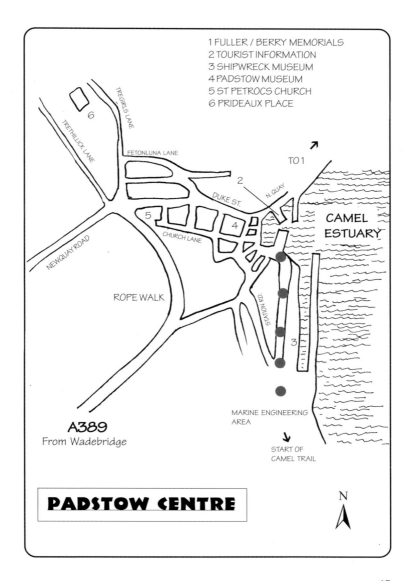

1 FULLER / BERRY MEMORIALS
2 TOURIST INFORMATION
3 SHIPWRECK MUSEUM
4 PADSTOW MUSEUM
5 ST PETROCS CHURCH
6 PRIDEAUX PLACE

PADSTOW CENTRE

• **Rock** Just across the estuary from Padstow and connected by a shuttle ferry service. Known as the 'Beverley Hills' of North Cornwall because of the number of mansions built there.

ACCOMMODATION - PADSTOW

Heminsford House, 21 Grenville Road (01841) 532806 £££-PL-DR-SEC-WKSH. 0.5 miles.
Kellacott, 29 Church St (01841) 532851. £££-DR-LAU-SEC-WKSH. Near route.
Roselyn, 20 Grenville Rd (01841) 532756. Easter-Oct. £££/£-SEC. 0.7 miles.
Cyntwell, 4 Cross St. (01841) 532364. £££/£-LAU-SEC. 0.25 miles from route.
Beau Vista, Sarahs Lane (01841) 533270. ££££/£-DR-LAU-SEC-Basic tools. 0.5 miles.
Sable's House, 76 Sarah's View (01841) 533358. April - Sept. ££££-PL-LAU-SEC-WKSH. 0.5 miles.

Also try: Althea Library (01841) 532717. Lantern House (01841) 532566. Ambleside (01841) 532443. Captain's Cottage (01841) 533419. Khandalla (01841) 532961

Λ **Dennis Cove Camping**, Padstow (01841) 532349. Easter-Sept. **Trerethen Touring Park**, Padstow (01841) 532061. 1st April-Oct.

Peaceful contemplation on the Camel Trail, overlooking the estuary (section 1)

Padstow's maritime tradition -
a wooden bowsprit in the harbour
(section 1)

Camel Trail - estuary is followed by leafy beauty (section 1)

PADSTOW - OTHER INFORMATION

Tourist Information Red Brick Building, North Quay (01841) 533449
Early Closing Wednesday
Hospital The Surgery, Boyd Avenue (01841) 532346
Banks Midland, Market Place (cashpoint). Lloyds, Duke St. (internal cashpoint). Barclays, Duke St. (cashpoint).
Brinhams Cycle Hire, South Quay (01841) 532594. Padstow Cycle Hire, South Quay (01841) 533533. Small stock of spares but their main business is cycle hire.

PADSTOW TO BODMIN

• On **Dennis Hill,** near the Camel Trail, a monument commemorates Queen Victoria.
• The **Camel Trail** follows the former London and South Western Railway. The **Iron Bridge** was a spectacular finale for the Atlantic Coast Express as it arrived in Padstow from Waterloo. **Camel and Penquean Quarries**, now defunct rock piles, provided flagstones and roof slates. **Wading birds** gather on the estuary seasonally.
• **Wadebridge** (Map pg 22) Former **port** with quays still lining the River Camel. Bridge dates from 15th century and is 320ft long with seventeen arches. Former Bodmin and Wadebridge rail station on Southern Way now houses the **John Betjeman Centre**. The railway took sand to Bodmin Moor to neutralise acid soil and brought clay and granite back. Numerous cycle hire outlets / shops in Wadebridge. Bridge Bike Hire, Eddystone Rd. (01208) 813050. Camel Trail Cycle Hire, Trevanson St. (01208) 814104. Babes & Bikes, 9 Polmorla Walk (01208) 815262. Tourist information in Town Hall (01208) 813725

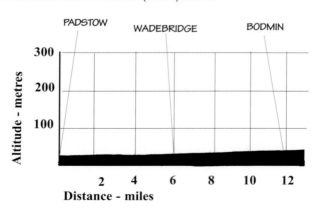

• The **Camel Trail** abruptly changes to pass through a narrow wooded valley alongside the river floodplain and several former station platforms. Camel Trail Tearooms just before Nanstallon Halt.
• The western terminus of the **Bodmin and Wenford Railway** is passed at Boscarne Junction shortly before the track splits with a link route to Bodmin on the right. This steam-operated line runs to Bodmin General Station and on to Bodmin Parkway with a spur line to Boscarne Junction. Services vary widely according to season. (01208) 73666. Pub food at the **Borough Arms** just off the Bodmin link path.

PADSTOW TO BODMIN - ACCOMMODATION

The Mowhay, Bodieve, Wadebridge (01208) 814078. £££-PL-DR-LAU-SEC-WKSH. 0.8 miles off route.

In Wadebridge also try: The Elms (01208) 814267. Inglenook (01208) 814847. Lavinleigh (01208) 812732. 7 Trevanson Rd. (01208) 815571. Spring Gardens (01208) 813771

△ **Little Bodieve Holiday Park**, Wadebridge (01208) 812323. 1st April - 31st Oct.

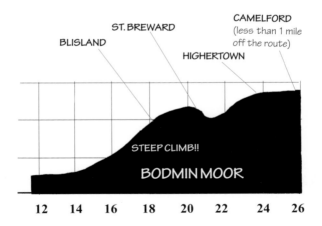

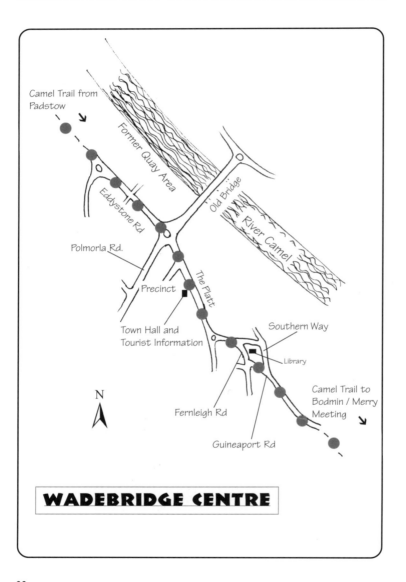

Camel Trail from Padstow

Former Quay Area

Eddystone Rd

Old Bridge

River Camel

Polmorla Rd.

Precinct

The Platt

Town Hall and Tourist Information

Southern Way

Library

N

Fernleigh Rd

Camel Trail to Bodmin / Merry Meeting

Guineaport Rd

WADEBRIDGE CENTRE

BODMIN - HISTORY AND ATTRACTIONS

• Claims to be the capital of Cornwall over Truro. Town centre 2km off the route.
• Elegant **Shire Hall** (former Assize Courts) and **Shire House** (former Judges' Lodgings) in Mount Folly Square.
• Bodmin's history is explored at the **Town Museum**, Mount Folly Square. April - Oct. (01208) 74159
• **Turret Clock** Marks execution spot of town mayor for participation in the 1549 Prayer Book Rising against new English translation of previous Latin bible.
• **Beacon Hill** 160 ft hill crowned with a 144 ft obelisk to General Walter Raleigh Gilbert, a local given a baronetcy for distinguished service in India. Easterly walk from town centre with great views. Surrounding area is being developed as a nature reserve.
• **Regimental Museum** Relics and history of the Duke of Cornwall's Light Infantry. The Keep, St. Nicholas St. Admission fee. Open July and Aug. (01208) 72810
• **Bodmin Gaol** Exhibition of prison life in the former county prison; an imposing building. Last hanging in the gaol was in 1909 and a crowd of 20,000 once attended the hanging of the 'Rough Tor Murderer'. Daily 10-6. Restaurant. Berrycombe Rd. Admission fee. (01208) 76292
• **St. Petroc's** is the largest parish church in Cornwall. 6th century Guron's Well in churchyard. Also in churchyard is **St. Thomas Becket's Chapel,** a 14th century chantry used as a school until the 1800s.

BODMIN - ACCOMMODATION

(Bodmin is on a spur, 1.5 miles from Camel Trail)

Trebay, 8 Cross Lane (01208) 73007. £££/££(price increase June-August)-PL-DR-LAU-SEC. 0.3 miles from Bodmin centre.
Orana Guest House, 3 Berrycombe Hill (01208) 77715. ££/£-DR-LAU-SEC-Some tools. Very near the link trail entering Bodmin from the Camel Trail.
Cromarty, 11 Priory Rd (01208) 74691. £££-PL-DR-SEC-Basic tools. Near centre.

Also try: Hotel Casi Casa (01208) 77592. Dunmere View (01208) 76482. 42 Boxwell Park (01208) 73009.

Ａ Camping & Caravan Club, Old Callywith Rd. Bodmin. (01208) 73834. March - Nov.

BODMIN - OTHER INFORMATION

Tourist Information Shire House, Mount Folly Square (01208) 76616.
Early Closing Wednesday
Hospital East Cornwall Hospital, Rhind St. (01208) 77771
Banks Barclays, Midland, NatWest and Lloyds all have town centre branches with cashpoints
🚲 The Bike Shop, Church Square (01208) 72557

BODMIN TO CAMELFORD

• **Bodmin Moor** The short section along the edge of the moor takes in a huge range of surreal scenery, almost lunar- like in places. Gorse bushes give way to boulder-strewn fields and finally the eerie flats of Davidstow Moor. All the while the rocky summits, or tors, at the centre of the moor provide a stunning backdrop. Grazing wild ponies add to the uniqueness of the area. Old runways and building remains indicate the site of an old wartime airfield on Davidstow Moor. The granite moorland contains Cornwall's two highest points; Brown Willy and Rough Tor.
• Shortly after finishing the Camel Trail comes the unique granite village of **Blisland**. Manor house and old inn are complemented by the unusually dedicated church of St. Protus and St. Hyacinth (brothers, martyred in Italy) with perhaps the finest rood screen in the country in a truly breathtaking interior. Impressive **Jubilee Rock** is a granite boulder with coats of arms carved into it. About 1 mile north of Blisland and off the route (ask directions).
• At over 200 metres (720 ft) **St. Breward** is Cornwall's highest village, historically based on quarrying. The moorland hereabouts is littered with prehistoric hut and stone circles and stripple stones. Nearby De Lank quarries provided granite for Blackfriars Bridge in London and Eddystone and Beachy Head lighthouses. **The Old Inn** has full bar and A La Carte menus. 12-2 & 6.30-9 (8.30 in winter), Sharps and Ruddles real ales.
• Near Highertown and Watergate the route passes underneath **Roughtor**, the second highest point in Cornwall and the destination for lots of trippers.

BODMIN TO CAMELFORD - ACCOMMODATION

Lower Helland Farm, Helland Bridge (01208) 72813. £££-DR-SEC-WKSH. Near route.
Lavethan, Blisland (01208) 850487. £££-DR-LAU-SEC. 0.5 miles.
Trevissick Farm, Blisland (01208) 850227. Closed December. £££-PL-DR-LAU-SEC-WKSH. 1 mile.

Also try: Tarny, St. Breward (01208) 850583. Treswallock Fm. (01208) 850255. In Blisland enquire at the Old Inn for local B&Bs. (01208) 850711.

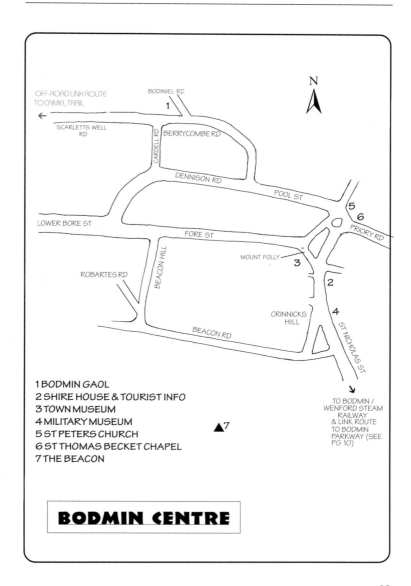

OFF-ROAD LINK ROUTE
TO CAMEL TRAIL

BODINIEL RD

1

SCARLETTS WELL
RD

CARDELL RD

BERRYCOMBE RD

N

DENNISON RD

POOL ST

5
6

LOWER BORE ST

FORE ST

PRIORY RD

MOUNT FOLLY

3

ROBARTES RD

BEACON HILL

2

4

CRINNICKS
HILL

ST NICHOLAS ST

BEACON RD

1 BODMIN GAOL
2 SHIRE HOUSE & TOURIST INFO
3 TOWN MUSEUM
4 MILITARY MUSEUM
5 ST PETERS CHURCH
6 ST THOMAS BECKET CHAPEL
7 THE BEACON

▲7

TO BODMIN /
WENFORD STEAM
RAILWAY
& LINK ROUTE
TO BODMIN
PARKWAY (SEE
PG 10)

BODMIN CENTRE

25

CAMELFORD - HISTORY AND ATTRACTIONS

• Inhabitants of Camelford claim it is the site of **King Arthur's last battle** (against his rebellious nephew Mordred). Now firmly on the tourist map at the centre of 'King Arthur Country'.

• **North Cornwall Museum** Displays on all aspects of Cornish life. Has won an award as Britain's best small museum. 1st April-30th Sept. Admission fee. (01840) 212954.

• **Town Hall** sports a camel-shaped weather vane and is now the town library.

• There are two **Methodist chapels** The Free Methodist Chapel on Market St. was the result of a group of breakaway Methodists rebelling against the establishment.

• Pleasant walks by the river Camel and through **Enfield Park**.

• The **Indian King Arts Centre** records the 18th century arrival in Camelford of a Cherokee Indian king and his family.

• Some miles off the route (one mile north of Camelford on the Boscastle Rd) is the **Museum of Historic Cycling** Enthusiasts may wish to make a detour here. Over 400 cycles and other memorabilia. Sun - Thurs. all year. Admission charge. (01840) 212811

CAMELFORD - ACCOMMODATION

The Countryman Hotel, 7 Victoria Road (01840) 212250 £££ to £££££. PL-DR-SEC-WKSH. 1.5 miles off route.

Trenarth, Victoria Road (01840) 213295. ££/£-PL-DR-SEC-WKSH. 1.5 miles.

Masons Arms Pub (01840) 213309. £££-PL-DR-LAU-SEC. 1.5 miles. Meals 12-2.30 & 6-9. St Austell beer.

Silver Moon, Lane End (01840) 213736. Snacks-Easter to Oct. £££-PL-DR-LAU-SEC-WKSH.

Penlea House, Station Road (01840) 212194. ££/£-DR-LAU-SEC-WKSH.

Also try: Chywartha (01840) 212969. Kings Acre (01840) 213561.

⚠ **Juilots Well Holiday Park**, Camelford (01840) 213302. May - Sept. **Kings Acre**, Camelford (01840) 213561. May - Oct.

CAMELFORD - OTHER INFORMATION

Tourist Information The Clease (01840) 212954. Housed in the North Cornwall Museum. Seasonal.

Early Closing Wednesday

Hospital Camelford Medical Centre, nr St. Thomas' Church (01840) 213894/3

Banks Lloyds, Barclays and Natwest Banks (last two with cashpoints) on or near Market St.

Camel weathervane at Camelford Town Hall (section 1)

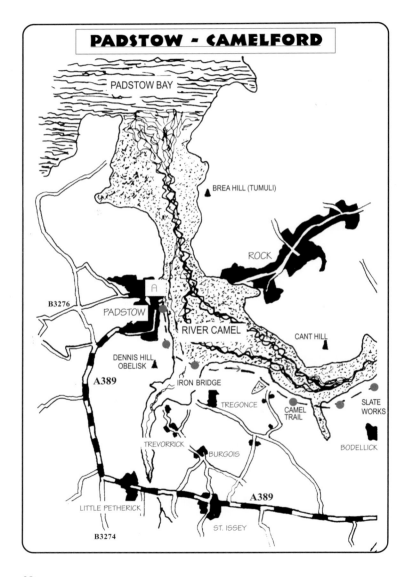

PADSTOW - CAMELFORD

PADSTOW BAY

BREA HILL (TUMULI)

ROCK

B3276

A

PADSTOW

RIVER CAMEL

CANT HILL

DENNIS HILL
OBELISK

A389

IRON BRIDGE

TREGONCE

CAMEL
TRAIL

SLATE
WORKS

TREVORRICK

BURGOIS

BODELLICK

LITTLE PETHERICK

A389

ST. ISSEY

B3274

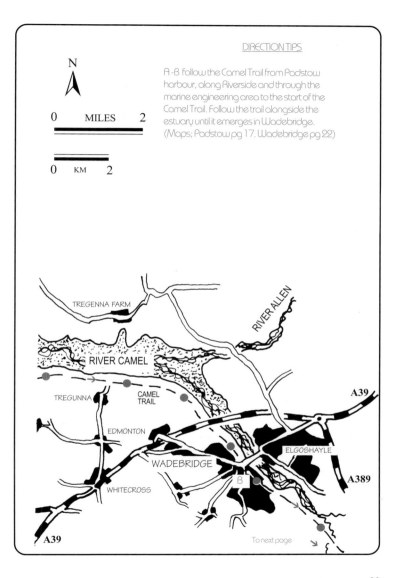

DIRECTION TIPS

A - At the split keep left on main trail for Poley's Bridge. For detour to Bodmin centre go right.

B - After passing under the A389 keep on the level trail, ignoring any turnings to left and right that descend or ascend.

C - On meeting the road at Merry Meeting you leave the Camel Trail. Go right to a road T-junction. At this junction go left for St. Breward and Blisland. Immediately there is a split - go right to begin the steepish climb towards Blisland.

D - On entering Blisland left by telephone box and keep to left side of green. Take the left hand most turn and exit Blisland past a small housing estate. Follow signs for St. Breward at subsequent junctions.

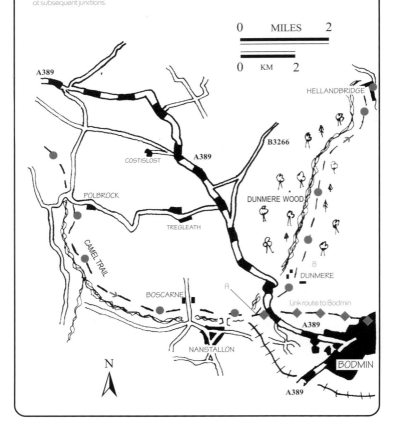

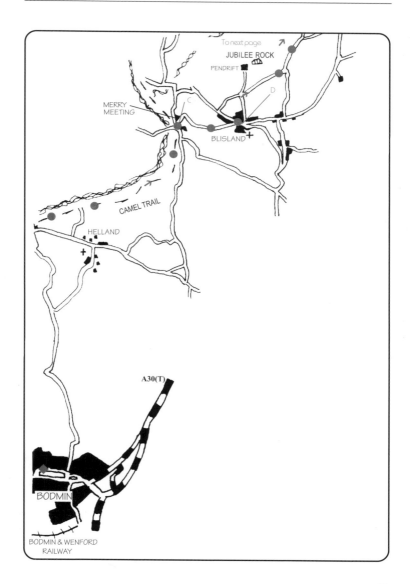

To next page

JUBILEE ROCK

PENDRIFT

D

MERRY
MEETING

C

BLISLAND

CAMEL TRAIL

HELLAND

A30(T)

BODMIN

BODMIN & WENFORD
RAILWAY

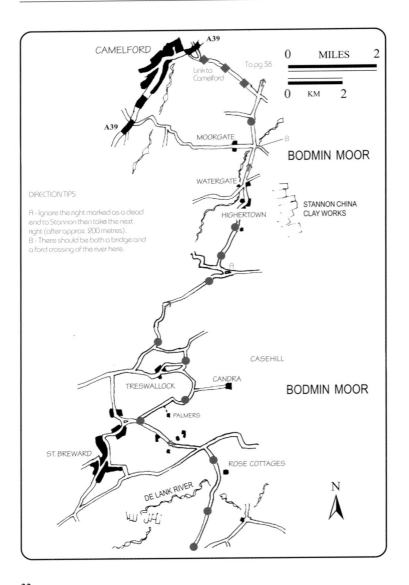

CAMELFORD

A39

To pg 38

Link to
Camelford

A39

0   MILES   2

0   KM   2

MOORGATE

B

BODMIN MOOR

WATERGATE

STANNON CHINA
CLAY WORKS

HIGHERTOWN

DIRECTION TIPS

A - Ignore the right marked as a dead
end to Stannon then take the next
right (after approx. 200 metres).
B - There should be both a bridge and
a ford crossing of the river here.

A

CASEHILL

CANDRA

BODMIN MOOR

TRESWALLOCK

PALMERS

ST. BREWARD

ROSE COTTAGES

DE LANK RIVER

N

32

2 CAMELFORD - HOLSWORTHY

Section Distance 32 miles / 51.5 km   **Off-road** Small section near Bude

Accumulated Distance 58 miles / 93 km

The Route After leaving Bodmin Moor you head north through quiet countryside to meet some very tough riding on a precipitous coastal road, rewarded by fantastic views of this beautiful coastline. There is an easier if less spectacular inland alternative. Passing from Cornwall into North Devon after Bude the landscape becomes characteristically green and rolling before the stage ends at the attractive market town of Holsworthy.

CAMELFORD TO BUDE

• From Camelford the route descends towards Bude (though it has its ups and downs), passing the spectacular coastal scenery around **Millook** on the way. At **Millook Haven** the astonishingly contorted cliff strata of sandstone and shale tower above a small attractive cove, but note strong currents make bathing unsafe.
Bay View Inn Widemouth Bay; meals 12-2.30 & 6-9.30. Real ales.

CAMELFORD TO BUDE - ACCOMMODATION

Bay View Inn, Widemouth Bay (01288) 361273. ££/£-PL-SEC-Basic tools. On route.
Widemouth Manor, Widemouth Bay. (01288) 361263 £££-PL-DR-LAU-SEC-WKSH. On route.

Also try: Brocksmoor, Widemouth Bay (01288) 361207. Quinceborough Farm, Widemouth Bay (01288) 361236

BUDE - HISTORY AND ATTRACTIONS

• Famous as a **surfing centre** (the 'Bondi of Britain') due to its surrounding miles of golden sand and impressive breakers. Large sea-filled open air pool at the end of nearby Summerleaze Beach. With its large hotels on the Strand it also has the feel of a once affluent holiday resort.
• The sea lock is a remnant of **Bude Canal** which ran 35 miles to Launceston and rose 350 ft in 6 miles. It took sand inland to reduce the acidity of farmland. Tub-boats operated on it, achieving the height changes by negotiating large ramps on metal rails, the power here coming from various water contraptions. Traces of the old incline are evident further along the route at Marhamchurch.

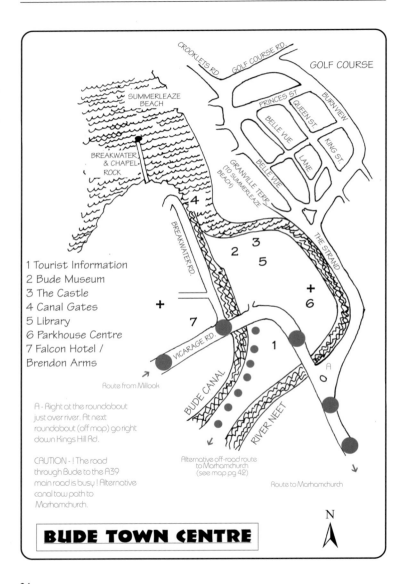

1 Tourist Information
2 Bude Museum
3 The Castle
4 Canal Gates
5 Library
6 Parkhouse Centre
7 Falcon Hotel /
Brendon Arms

Route from Millook

A - Right at the roundabout
just over river. At next
roundabout (off map) go right
down Kings Hill Rd.

CAUTION - ! The road
through Bude to the A39
main road is busy ! Alternative
canal tow path to
Marhamchurch.

Alternative off-road route
to Marhamchurch
(see map pg 42)

Route to Marhamchurch

BUDE TOWN CENTRE

N

• **Bude Castle**, now housing local council offices, was built by local inventor and scientist Sir Goldsworthy Gurney and was apparently constructed on shifting sands but actually sits on a concrete 'raft' and has clearly survived the test of time.

• A **folk exhibition** is housed in a former blacksmith's shop above the canal detailing the history of the 'wreckers', once notorious on this part of the coast, and canal background. April - Sept. Admission charge. (01288) 353576

• There are good walks over **Efford Down** to the west to the **Pepperpot**, a nineteenth century coastguard's lookout based on the Temple of the Winds in Athens. Another good stroll follows the breakwater to Chapel Rock, beyond which is an old bathing pool (low tide only - be careful crossing the breakwater).

• Get to the **Bude Marshes Nature Reserve** by walking down the canal towpath from behind the visitor centre to the bird hide.

BUDE - ACCOMMODATION

Dol Amroth Guest House, 23 Downs View (01288) 352202. £££-PL-DR-SEC. 0.75 miles from route.
Links Side Guest House, 7 Burn View (01288) 352410. ££/£-PL-DR-LAU-SEC-WKSH. 0.3 miles.
Fairway House, 8 Downs View (01288) 355059. £££-PL-DR-LAU-SEC. 0.75 miles.
Clovelleys House, 4 Burn View (01288) 352761. £££-PL-DR-LAU-WKSH. 0.3 miles.

Also try: Kimberley House (01288) 352342. Seabreeze (01288) 355922. Derril (01288) 353697.

⚠ **Bude Holiday Park**, Bude (01288) 355955

BUDE - OTHER INFORMATION

Tourist Information The Crescent (01288) 354240
Early Closing Thursday
Hospital Stratton Hospital, Bude (01288) 352161
Banks Lloyds, NatWest and Barclays found around The Triangle, between The Strand and Belle Vue. All have cashpoints.
🚲 Tracks, 20 Queen St. (01288) 356689. North Coast Cycles, Ocean View Road (01288) 352974.

BUDE TO HOLSWORTHY

• **Marhamchurch** is a rectangular shaped village set on a ridge above the surrounding farmland. Norman church has 15th century oak door and encased sanctuary knocker. Village has an interesting mix of architecture including a quaint Sunday School and Church of England Institute building.
• **Bridgerule** Clustered around a bridge over the Tamar. Some form of bridge has been here since Doomsday times. Bridge Inn serves meals.
• **Pyworthy** Good views from churchyard. Molesworth Arms serves meals.

BUDE TO HOLSWORTHY - ACCOMMODATION

Court Farm, Marhamchurch (01288) 361494. £££/£-PL-DR-LAU-SEC-Basic tools. On route. Opposite pub and with heated pool Easter-Nov!
Bullers Arms, Marhamchurch (01288) 361277. ££££-PL-DR-LAU-SEC-WKSH. On route. Pub meals 11.30-2.30 & 6-9.30. Wide range of real ales.
Holladon Farm, Bridgerule (01288) 381268. March-Oct. Evening meal. ££-PL-DR-LAU-SEC-WKSH. 1 mile from Derril.
Little Knowle Farm, Pyworthy nr Holsworthy (01409) 254642. £££-PL-DR-LAU-WKSHP. Near route. ⌂ Space for 2 tents.

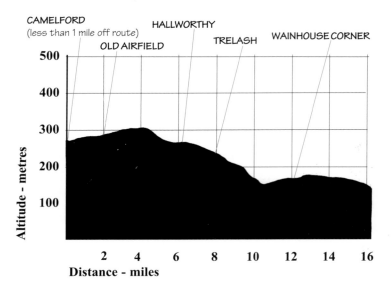

Also try: Lodgeworthy Farm, Bridgerule (01288) 381351. Northmoor Farm, Pyworthy (01288) 381467.

⚑ **Hedley Wood**, Nr. Bridgerule approx 2 miles from route. (01288) 381404.

Follow the sign!

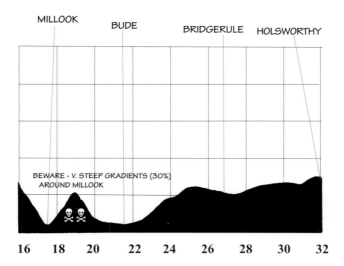

MILLOOK   BUDE   BRIDGERULE   HOLSWORTHY

BEWARE - V. STEEP GRADIENTS (30%) AROUND MILLOOK

16   18   20   22   24   26   28   30   32

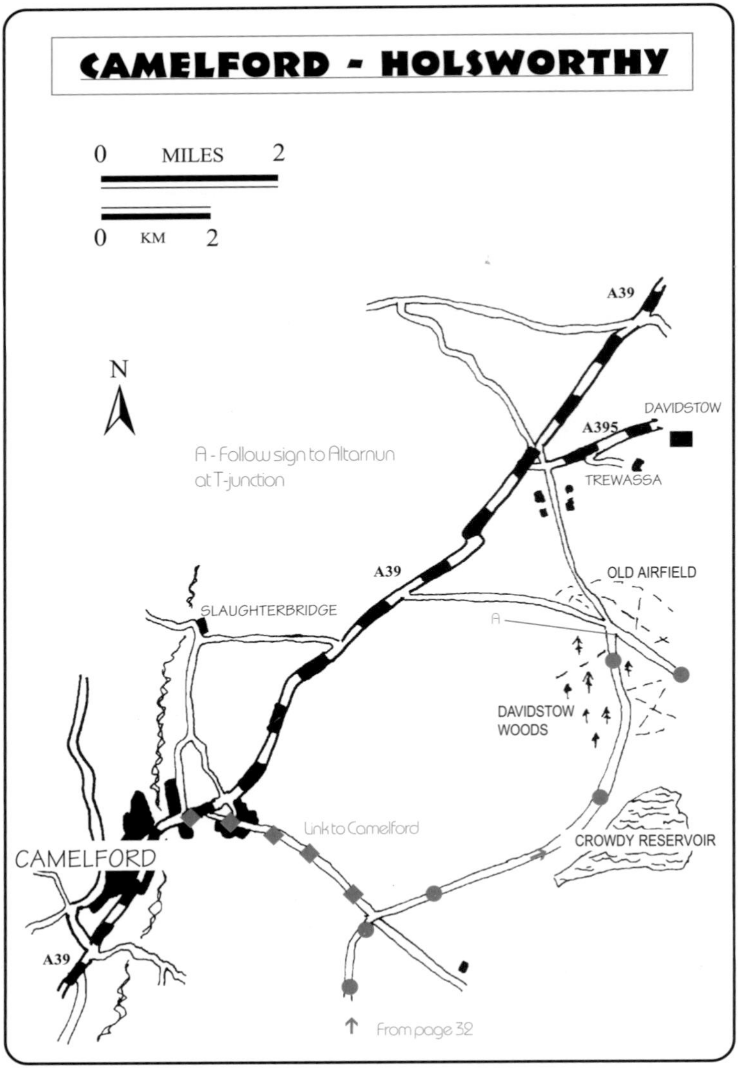

CAMELFORD - HOLSWORTHY

0   MILES   2

0   KM   2

N

A39

DAVIDSTOW

A - Follow sign to Altarnun
at T-junction

A395

TREWASSA

OLD AIRFIELD

A39

SLAUGHTERBRIDGE

A

DAVIDSTOW
WOODS

CROWDY RESERVOIR

CAMELFORD

Link to Camelford

A39

From page 32

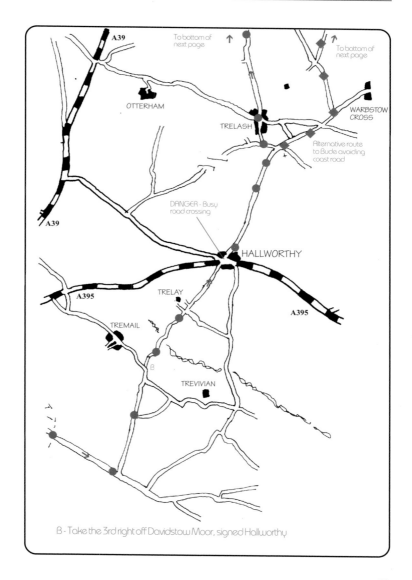

A39

To bottom of next page ↑

To bottom of next page ↑

OTTERHAM

WARBSTOW CROSS

TRELASH

Alternative route to Bude avoiding coast road

A39

DANGER - Busy road crossing

HALLWORTHY

A395

TRELAY

A395

TREMAIL

B

TREVIVIAN

B - Take the 3rd right off Davidstow Moor, signed Hallworthy

39

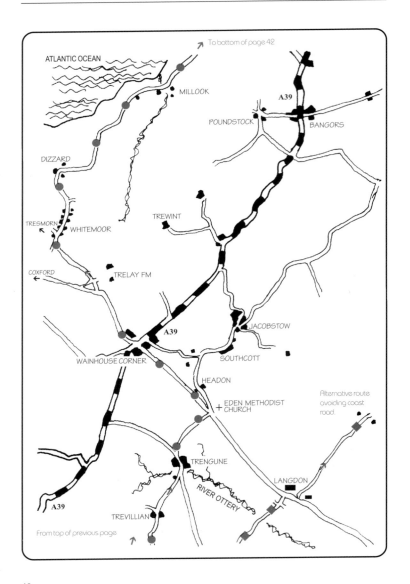

ATLANTIC OCEAN

MILLOOK

To bottom of page 42

A39

POUNDSTOCK

BANGORS

DIZZARD

TREWINT

TRESMORN

WHITEMOOR

COXFORD

TRELAY FM

JACOBSTOW

A39

SOUTHCOTT

WAINHOUSE CORNER

HEADON

+ EDEN METHODIST
  CHURCH

Alternative route
avoiding coast
road.

TRENGUNE

LANGDON

RIVER OTTERY

A39

TREVILLIAN

From top of previous page

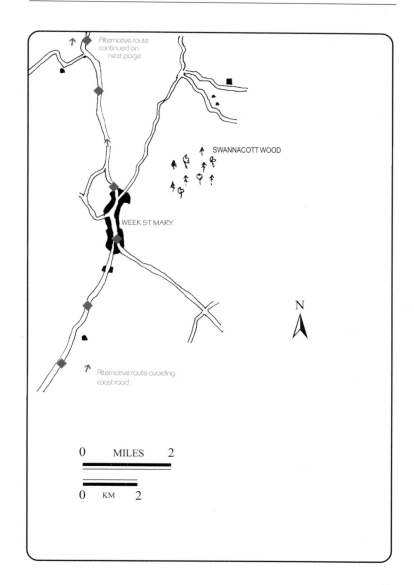

Alternative route
continued on
next page

SWANNACOTT WOOD

WEEK ST MARY

N

Alternative route avoiding
coast road.

0   MILES   2

0   KM   2

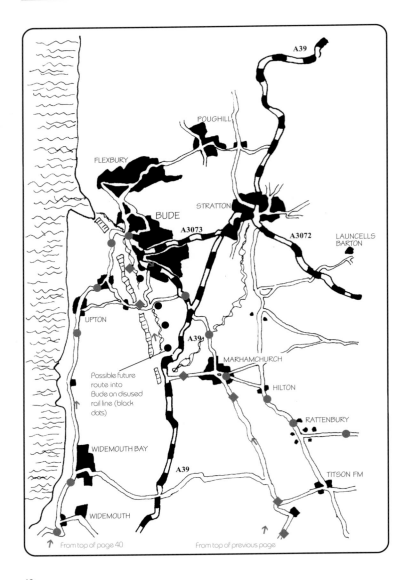

POUGHILL

FLEXBURY

BUDE

STRATTON

A3073

A3072

LAUNCELLS
BARTON

A39

UPTON

A39

MARHAMCHURCH

HILTON

Possible future
route into
Bude on disused
rail line (black
dots)

RATTENBURY

WIDEMOUTH BAY

A39

TITSON FM

WIDEMOUTH

↑ From top of page 40

From top of previous page ↑

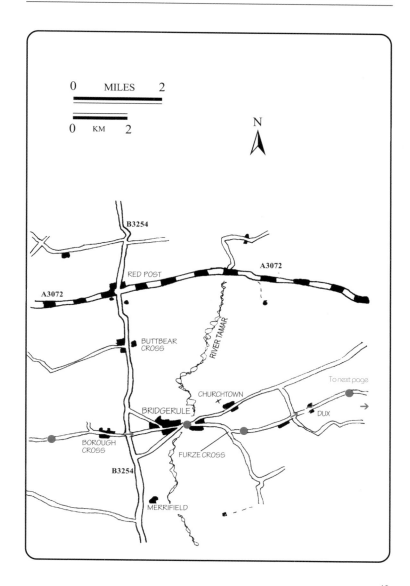

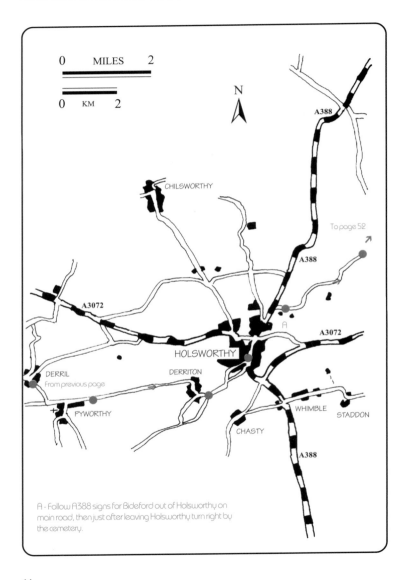

0 MILES 2

0 KM 2

N

A388

CHILSWORTHY

To page 52

A388

A3072

A3072

HOLSWORTHY

A

DERRIL
From previous page

DERRITON

PYWORTHY

WHIMBLE

STADDON

CHASTY

A388

A - Follow A388 signs for Bideford out of Holsworthy on
main road, then just after leaving Holsworthy turn right by
the cemetery.

3 HOLSWORTHY - BIDEFORD

Section Distance 29 miles / 46.5 km   **Off-road** 13 miles / 21km

Accumulated Distance 87 miles / 140 km

The Route Although the rolling green Devon countryside after Holsworthy looks idyllic and gentle there are numerous small dips and climbs with steep gradients, especially so between Cookbury and Black Torrington; be prepared for quite a physical challenge! The beautiful Tarka Trail, joined 15.5 miles (25km) after Holsworthy, is easy cycling through a beautiful combination of ancient valley woodland and the widening Torridge as it turns into a tidal estuary towards Bideford. The first view of Bideford from East-the-Water, across the Torridge, is quite striking; the old arched bridge leads to the quayside backed by brightly-coloured buildings and church spires.

HOLSWORTHY - HISTORY AND ATTRACTIONS

• **Market centre** for north-west Devon with attractive central square.
• Landmark is the **pinnacled granite tower** of Church of St. Peter and St. Paul.
• Small **local museum** in the manor offices. April - Oct. Weds only. Small charge.

HOLSWORTHY - ACCOMMODATION

Dormy House, Holsworthy (01409) 253634. April-Oct. £££-PL-DR-LAU-SEC-possible use of workshop. 2 miles from Holsworthy on main Holsworthy - Bude road.
Penrose Villa, Bodmin St (01409) 253693. £££-DR-SEC-WKSH. On route.
Forda Farm, Thornbury (01409) 261369. £££-PL-DR-LAU-SEC-WKSH. 1.5 miles from route.

Also try: Merrymead (01409) 253452)

HOLSWORTHY - OTHER INFORMATION

Tourist Information Manor car park (01409) 254185
Market Day Wednesday (including livestock market)
Early Closing Thursday
Hospital Holsworthy Health Centre (01409) 253692
Banks Midland (cashpoint), Lloyds, Barclays (cashpoint) and Natwest; all central.
🚲 Giffords, 12 Victoria Square (01409) 254020

Bude Canal approaching the sea lock (section 2)

Tarka Trail approaching Bideford (section 3)

HOLSWORTHY TO BIDEFORD

• After passing through the quiet villages of **Cookbury** and **Holemoor** you get glimpses of the hills rising towards Dartmoor away to your right. The real gem on this section is **Sheepwash** with its gorgeous central square, surrounded by thatched cottage, church and inn. **Half Moon Inn** Meals 12-2 (Restaurant only 8-9). Bar and restaurant meals. Courage and range of local ales.
• The **Tarka Trail** is part of the Tarka Trail regional route, based on the travels of Tarka the Otter in the book by Henry Williamson and houses a number of reminders of its former glory years as a railway and of the surrounding industrial activity. The long terrace of houses at **East Yarde** was built for workers at nearby clay mines. It also crosses several **spectacular viaducts** and passes former stations at Petrockstow, Dunsbeare and East-the-Water, in varying states of preservation (the latter has information centre, exhibition and refreshments served in converted carriage. 🚲 Torrington Cycle Hire, just after passing under A386, west of Great Torrington. (01805) 622633. **Puffing Billy Pub** Torrington Railway Station. Meals 12 - 2.30 & 7-11. Dartmoor and selected real ales. Family pub including tuck shop.
• **Great Torrington** affords superb views over the Devon countryside from its cliff top position. Town centre about 1 mile off the route. Pretty market square. Small museum in Town Hall. **Dartington Glass** has glass-blowing displays. Admission charge & refreshments. Opening details ring (01805) 624233. **Castle Hill** is a superb vantage point over the surrounding countryside and to the south-east. Near the river is an obelisk commemorating the battle of Waterloo.
• **Rosemoor Gardens** are a mile to the south-east of Great Torrington. Specialise in roses. Over 40 acres. April - Oct. daily. Admission charge & refreshments.

HOLSWORTHY TO BIDEFORD - ACCOMMODATION

Half Moon Inn, Sheepwash (01409) 231376 . £££££-PL-DR-LAU-SEC. On route.
Burnards, Weare Giffard (Between Torrington and Bideford) (01237) 473809. March - Sept inclusive. £££-DR-LAU-SEC. Near Tarka Trail.
The Cyder Presse, Weare Giffard (01237) 425517. £££-PL-DR-LAU-SEC. Bar meals also available. Near Tarka Trail.
Riversdale, Weare Giffard (01237) 423676. ££££-PL-DR-LAU-SEC. Near Tarka Trail.

Also try: Smytham Manor, Little Torrington (01805) 622110. 0.3 miles from Tarka Trail.

⛺ **Old Mill House**, Cookbury (very basic) (01409) 281379. **Smytham Manor**, Little Torrington. (01805) 622110. 0.3 miles from Tarka Trail.

BIDEFORD - HISTORY AND ATTRACTIONS

• Long tree-lined **17th century harbour**, once one of the busiest in England, is still used today by coasters and small ships from the continent. The town also has some fine **medieval streets** such as Gunstone and Buttgarden. Bridgeland St. contains striking 17th century merchants' houses.

• **24 arched bridge** has spanned the Torridge since medieval times and is still one of the town's best known landmarks at 677 ft long. Each arch is a different size.

• **Bideford Railway Museum** is housed in the former station, next to the Tarka Trail. Afternoons, Sun, Tues and Bank Holidays.

• The parish church has interesting memorial plaque to **Sir Richard Grenville** who helped found the American colonies in the 16th century. He died off the Azores fighting Spanish galleons. He brought the first North American Indian to reach England. The Grenville chantry also lies within the church.

• **Appledore** is a fishing port just north of Bideford and is famous for its shipyards. There is a good panorama of it from section 4, on the Tarka Trail. Evocative narrow streets with bow-fronted cottages and fine houses. **North Devon Maritime Museum** Local boat building, smuggling, Viking raids and Tudor expeditions are all covered here. Odun House, Odun Road, Appledore. Easter - Sept. Admission charge.

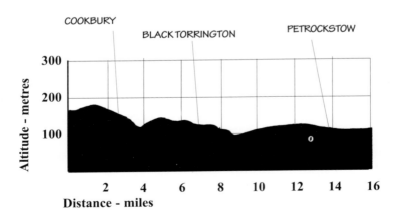

• **Boat trips to Lundy** leave from the Quay area. Lundy is Norse for Puffin Island. Walk the island's three mile length and sample the abundant wildlife. (01237) 470422 for sailing details.

• **Burton Art Gallery** Gallery and museum housing works by Reynolds and novel bone model ships made by French prisoners of war.

• Famous novelist **Charles Kingsley** (*The Water Babies)* lived and worked here. Look for his statue by the car park.

• In **East-the -Water**, on the eastern side of the Torridge, lies **Chudleigh Fort**, built when Barnstaple and Bideford sided with Parliament against the King in the Civil War. Subsequently purchased as a war memorial and laid out as a public park. The **Royal Hotel** is a good place to stop for coffee; inside is a 17th century house!

BIDEFORD - ACCOMMODATION

Corner House, The Strand (01237) 473722. £££-PL-SEC.

Also try: Torridge Vale (01237) 474481. Ellerton (01237) 473352. 13 Park Avenue (01237) 470007. Burscott House (01237) 478262. Joiners Arms (01237) 472675

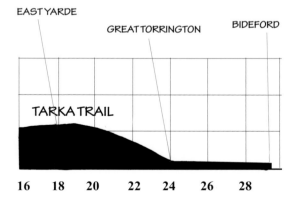

EAST YARDE

GREAT TORRINGTON   BIDEFORD

TARKA TRAIL

16   18   20   22   24   26   28

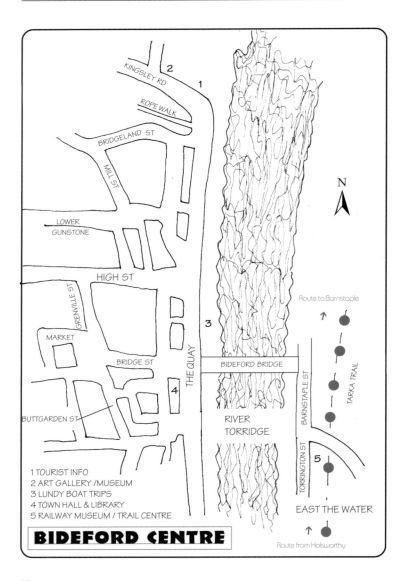

KINGSLEY RD

ROPE WALK

BRIDGELAND ST

MILL ST

LOWER GUNSTONE

HIGH ST

GRENVILLE ST

MARKET

BRIDGE ST

THE QUAY

BUTTGARDEN ST

BIDEFORD BRIDGE

RIVER TORRIDGE

N

Route to Barnstaple

BARNSTAPLE ST

TARKA TRAIL

TORRINGTON ST

EAST THE WATER

Route from Holsworthy

1 TOURIST INFO
2 ART GALLERY /MUSEUM
3 LUNDY BOAT TRIPS
4 TOWN HALL & LIBRARY
5 RAILWAY MUSEUM / TRAIL CENTRE

BIDEFORD CENTRE

BIDEFORD - OTHER INFORMATION

Tourist Information Near Victoria Park entrance. (01237) 477676
Market Days Tuesday and Saturday
Early Closing Wednesday
Hospital Bideford Hospital, Abbotsham Road (01237) 472692
Banks Barclays, Lloyds & NatWest all on High St. with cashpoints. Midland, The Quay (cashpoint).
🚲 Bideford Cycle Hire, Torrington St. East-the-Water (to the left of the Tarka Trail as you enter East-the-Water. (01237) 424123. Freebird, High St. (01237) 470791

Cliff strata at Millook (section 2)

51

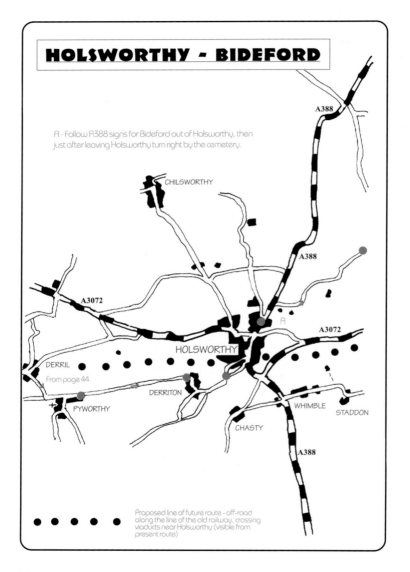

HOLSWORTHY - BIDEFORD

A - Follow A388 signs for Bideford out of Holsworthy, then just after leaving Holsworthy turn right by the cemetery.

A388

CHILSWORTHY

A388

A3072

A3072

HOLSWORTHY

DERRIL

From page 44

DERRITON

PYWORTHY

WHIMBLE

STADDON

CHASTY

A388

Proposed line of future route - off-road along the line of the old railway, crossing viaducts near Holsworthy (visible from present route)

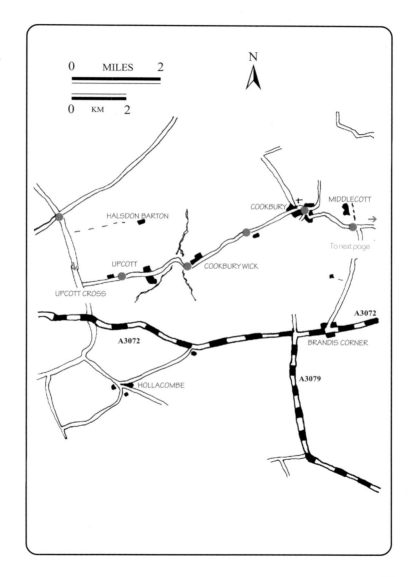

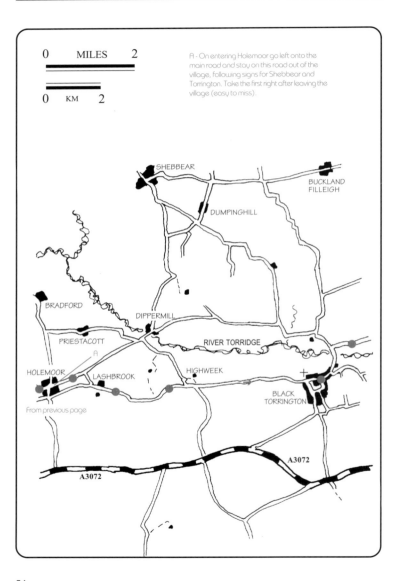

A - On entering Holemoor go left onto the main road and stay on this road out of the village, following signs for Shebbear and Torrington. Take the first right after leaving the village (easy to miss).

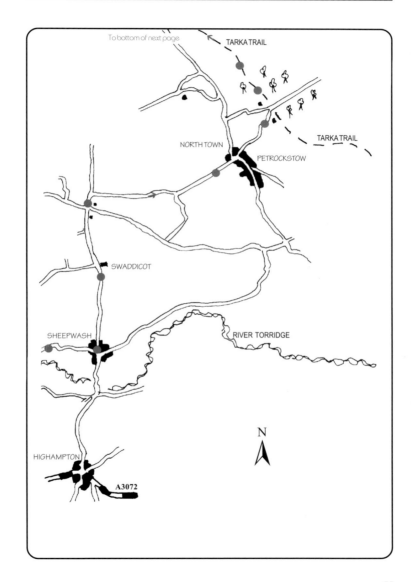

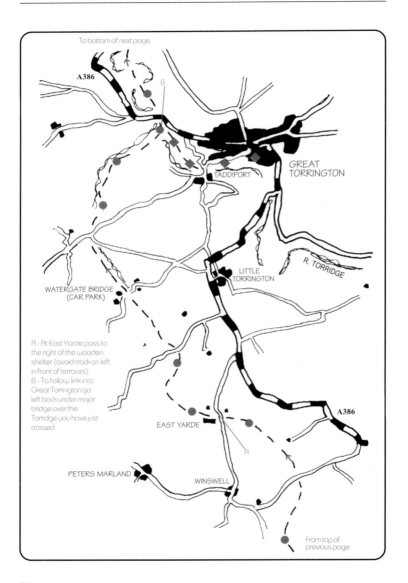

To bottom of next page

A386

B

GREAT
TORRINGTON

TADDIPORT

R. TORRIDGE

LITTLE
TORRINGTON

WATERGATE BRIDGE
(CAR PARK)

A - At East Yarde pass to
the right of the wooden
shelter (avoid track on left
in front of terraces)
B - To follow link into
Great Torrington go
left back under major
bridge over the
Torridge you have just
crossed.

A386

EAST YARDE

A

PETERS MARLAND

WINSWELL

From top of
previous page

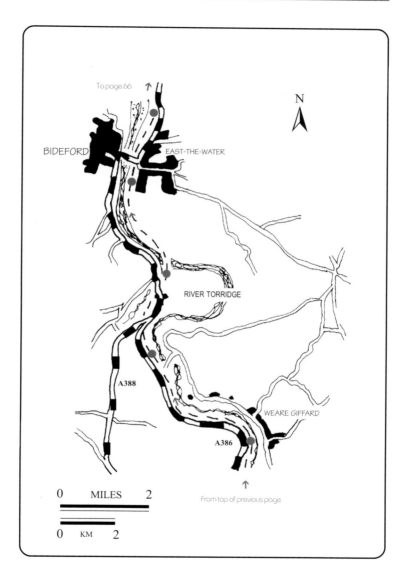

4 BIDEFORD - BRATTON FLEMING

Section Distance 20.5 miles / 33km   **Off-road** 11 miles / 17.5 km

Accumulated Distance 107.5 miles / 173km

The Route The Torridge estuary widens further to join the expansive Taw estuary across whose muddy waters lie a landscape of dunes (Braunton Burrows) and wide-open skies. Along the Torridge estuary the decaying hulls of boats lend an unusual charm. The route then passes through the suburbs of Barnstaple; the centre is well worth a short detour. A steep climb through several small settlements to the village of Bratton Fleming takes you to the edge of the Exmoor National Park.

BIDEFORD TO BARNSTAPLE

• **Tapeley Park** Less than a mile inland from Instow this William & Mary house is surrounded by Italian style gardens with pools and statues. Watch out for signs from the Tarka Trail. Easter to 1st Nov. Admission charge. (01271) 342371
• **Instow** is a small settlement behind a long, firm expanse of sand good for bathing. A ferry to Appledore operates from the small quay. Popular with artists for its grand views; Appledore and the Torridge estuary are backed by the Atlantic and the island of Lundy over 20 miles away. Preserved signal box open Sunday and Bank Holiday afternoons. ⊙ᛉᚱ Yelland Cycle Hire is by the Tarka Trail (01271) 861424

BIDEFORD TO BARNSTAPLE - ACCOMMODATION

Pilton Cottage, Victoria Terrace, Marine Parade, Instow (01271) 860202. £££-DR-SEC. 0.3miles from route.
Instow Youth Hostel, Worlington House, New Rd. Instow (01271) 860394. £-DR-LAU-SEC. YHA members only. Closed Sunday & Monday off-season. 0.3 miles.

Also try: Anchorage Hotel, Instow (01271) 860655. 1 Ballards Crescent, Yelland (01271) 861126.

On the Tarka Trail between Bideford and Barnstaple (section 4)

BARNSTAPLE - HISTORY AND ATTRACTIONS

• Busy market town and touring centre. Every summer the town is covered with floral displays for the 'Britain in Bloom' contest.

• Fine architecture, most notably **Queen Anne's Walk**, a colonnaded walkway where maritime trade once took place. The **Tome Stone**, where deals were made, can still be seen. Money was placed on top and the bargain publicly witnessed.

• 14th century **St. Anne's Chapel**, now a museum of local antiquities. Small but with a very interesting history including possible use by St. Sabinus, chantry chapel, grammar school and a place of worship for French Protestants. Parish church has twisted wooden spire.

• The old **castle** shows the remains of a Norman motte and bailey construction plus some later stone walls.

• The sixteen-arched **long bridge** over the Taw has been rebuilt several times.

• **Pannier Market** Impressive building with a beautiful roof.

• **Museum of North Devon** Natural, military and agricultural history amongst other topics, all connected with North Devon. Tues - Sat. (01271) 346747

• The **cattle market** is near the castle (Friday mornings).

• **North Devon Athenaeum** is a reading room with interesting collections given by local benefactor W.F.Rock. and also houses the above museum.

• **Jungleland** includes exotic plants such as cacti, rubber plants and cheese plants. (01271) 343884

• Trips to **Lundy** leave from the quay. Lundy is Norse for Puffin Island. Walk the island's three mile length and sample the abundant wildlife. (01237) 470422 for sailing details.

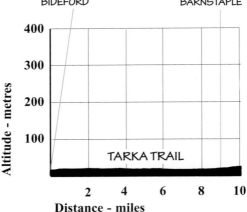

BARNSTAPLE - ACCOMMODATION

Try:

Crossways, Braunton Rd. (01271) 379120
Ivy House, Victoria Rd. (01271) 371198
Mulberry House, Barbican Terrace (01271) 345387
Nelson House, Newport Rd. (01271) 345929
West Lyn, Braunton Rd. (01271) 372778
West View, Pilton Causeway (01271) 326960
Hoopers End, Goodleigh Rd. (01271) 328363 / 373473
Kingston House, Runsam Rd. (01271) 373957
Mount Sandford, Landkey Rd. (01271) 342353

⚠ **Midland Caravan Park**, Braunton Road (01271) 43691. April - Sept.

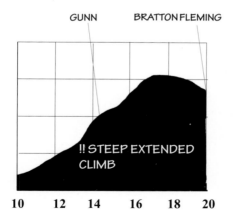

BARNSTAPLE - OTHER INFORMATION

Tourist Information 36 Boutport St. (01271) 375000
Market Days Tuesday and Friday
Early Closing Wednesday
Hospital North Devon Hospital, A39 Lynton Road. (01271) 322577
Banks Barclays, Boutport St. NatWest, High St. Lloyds, Cross St. Midland, High St. All have cashpoints.
🚲 Cyril Webber, Bear St. (01271) 343277. Rolle Quay Cycle Hire, Rolle Quay (01271) 345182. Cycle Centre, Barum Arcade (01271) 343869. No Sweat Bicycle Co. 23 Boutport St. (01271) 372660 Also a bike hire outlet at the train station as you enter the town on the Tarka Trail.

BARNSTAPLE TO BRATTON FLEMING - ACCOMMODATION

Try:

Willesleigh House, Goodleigh (01271) 346460 **Stone Fm**, Gunn (01271) 830473 **Kimbland Fm**, Near Brayford (01598) 710352 **Haxton Down Farm**, Bratton Fleming (01598) 710275 **Bracken House Hotel**, Bratton Fleming (01598) 710320 **Bragan**, Bratton Fleming (01598) 710457

⚠ **Brightlycott Fm**. Roborough (01271) 850330

Across the heather of Exmoor (section 5)

A - Pass Tescos and go through the underpass then emerge to bear right to a mini-roundabout. Pick up the cycle lane to the left. Immediately after the second entrance to Barton Rd go down the cycle path then bear right to climb to the top of Woodland Close. Left here and after passing Larkspur Gardens and Kestrel Way pick up the cycle path to emerge onto a very minor road. Go left and immediately at the next T-junction right signed for Willesleigh and Adland.

RIVER YEO

TOWN CENTRE

RIVER TAW

BARBICAN RD

BARTON RD

STATION RD

EASTERN AVENUE

A

B3233

HOLLOW TREE RD

TESCO

DIY STORE

STATION

LEISURE CENTRE

LANDKEY RD

SCHOOL

N

SCHOOL

LOVERS WALK

TAWTON RD

RUMSAN RD

BYPASS

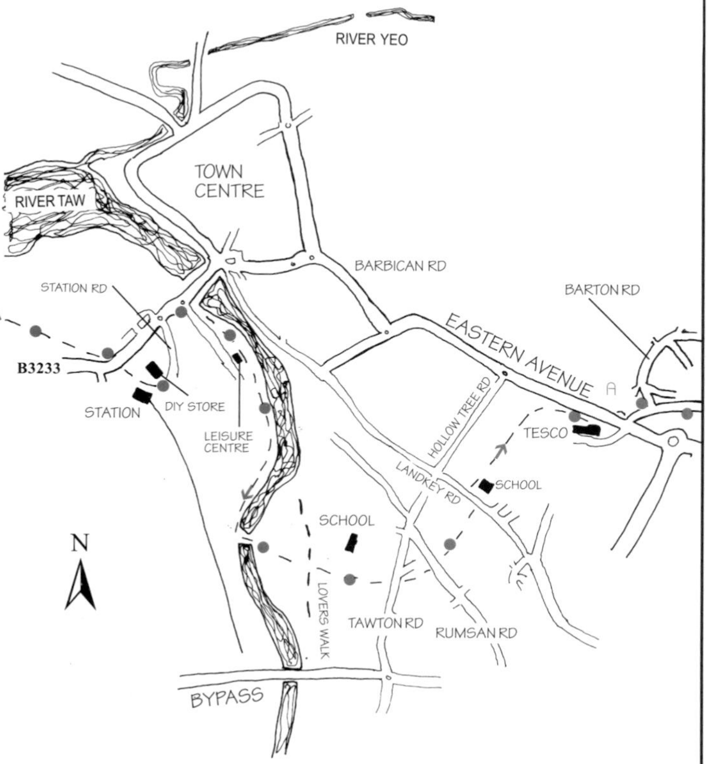

ROUTE AROUND BARNSTAPLE

N

ROLLE ST

RIVER YEO

NORTH WALK

VICARAGE ST

GAMMON WALK

HIGH ST

JOY ST

BOUTPORT ST

4

2

BEAR ST

CASTLE ST

HOLLAND WALK

BUTCHERS ROW

1

RIVER TAW

3

5

THE STRAND

QUEEN ST

THE SQUARE

6

LONG BRIDGE

TAW VALE

See previous page for
route around Barnstaple

1 TOURIST INFORMATION
2 PANNIER MARKET
3 ST ANNE'S CHAPEL
4 CASTLE MOUND
5 QUEEN ANNE'S WALK
6 ATHENAEUM / LIBRARY
& MUSEUM OF NORTH DEVON

BARNSTAPLE CENTRE

Typical hedging under construction on the climb away from Barnstaple (section 4)

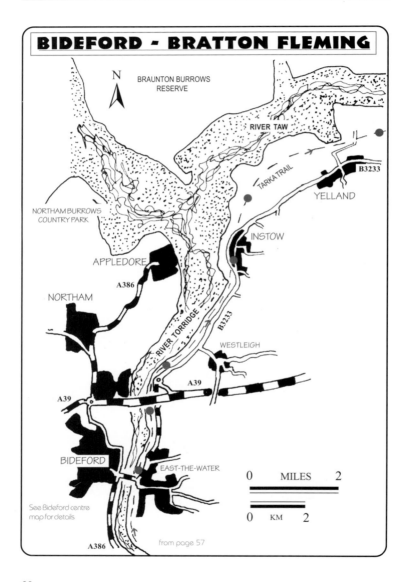

BIDEFORD - BRATTON FLEMING

N

BRAUNTON BURROWS
RESERVE

RIVER TAW

TARKA TRAIL

B3233

YELLAND

NORTHAM BURROWS
COUNTRY PARK

INSTOW

APPLEDORE

A386

NORTHAM

RIVER TORRIDGE

B3233

WESTLEIGH

A39

A39

BIDEFORD

EAST-THE-WATER

See Bideford centre
map for details

A386

from page 57

| 0 | MILES | 2 |

| 0 | KM | 2 |

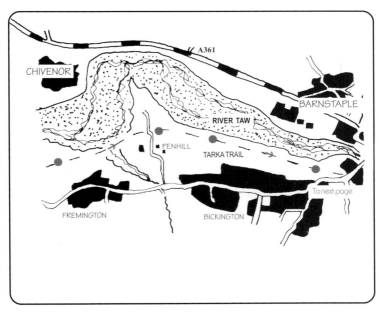

Instow signal box on the Tarka Trail (section 4)

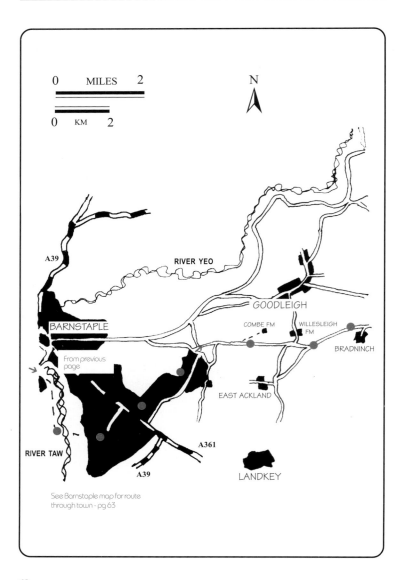

0   MILES   2

0   KM   2

N

A39

RIVER YEO

GOODLEIGH

COMBE FM

WILLESLEIGH FM

BRADNINCH

BARNSTAPLE

From previous page

EAST ACKLAND

RIVER TAW

A361

A39

LANDKEY

See Barnstaple map for route through town - pg 63

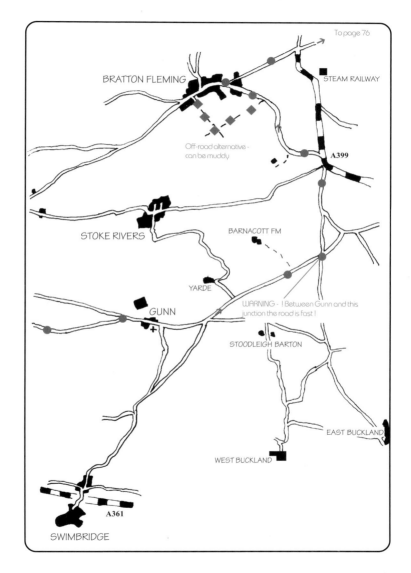

To page 76

BRATTON FLEMING

STEAM RAILWAY

Off-road alternative -
can be muddy

A399

STOKE RIVERS

BARNACOTT FM

YARDE

GUNN

WARNING - ! Between Gunn and this
junction the road is fast !

STOODLEIGH BARTON

EAST BUCKLAND

WEST BUCKLAND

A361

SWIMBRIDGE

5 BRATTON FLEMING - DULVERTON

Section Distance 21 miles / 34 km   **Off-road** 0 miles

Accumulated Distance 128.5 miles / 207 km

The Route A further contrast in scenery is provided in this section, the majority of which passes through Exmoor National Park. After a drop and a climb past Fullaford much of the route is relatively level before the final descent into the lovely village of Dulverton. The moorland scenery, backed by rolling green fields and valleys, has echoes of the Peak District about it, but the Taw Estuary in the distance makes it clear you are not in Derbyshire! Be prepared for relatively cooler weather and possibly stronger winds as you experience the highest point on the whole route on Fyldon Common. If you are planning to stay around the Exmoor National Park it is as well to make sure you book accommodation well in advance; it is a sparsely settled area and B&Bs can be few and far between (especially in summer time).

BRATTON FLEMING TO DULVERTON

• Much of **Exmoor** is now designated a National Park which aims to protect and manage its high, wild moorland, rolling green pastures, chequerboard fields and deep combes (small valleys). Originally one of the five ancient royal forests of Britain it was largely deforested in the nineteenth century and reverted to wasteland then was subsequently developed for agriculture. Wildlife lovers should look out for red deer and the tiny Exmoor pony which roam the tops. Tumuli, barrows and earthworks are found all over Exmoor. The main literary association of the area is R.D. Blackmore's Lorna Doone, based on the Doone outlaws who supposedly once operated in these remote parts.
• **Exmoor Wildlife Park** Specialising in small and endangered species. Admission charge. (01598) 763352
• **Exmoor Steam Railway** is on the route. Highest narrow gauge railway in England. Admission charge. Varied seasonal opening - ring (01598) 710711

BRATTON FLEMING TO DULVERTON - ACCOMMODATION

Barkham, Sandyway, South Molton (01643) 831370. £££/£-PL-DR-LAU-WKSH. Very near route.
Down Farm, Brayford (01598) 710683. ££/£-PL-DR-SEC-WKSH. 1.5 miles from route but free lift to/from route if required.

Also try: Sportsman Inn, Sandyway (01643) 831109 B&B and △. Scatterbrook Farm, Hinam Cross (01398) 323857. Hinam Farm, Hinam Cross (01398) 323405.

DULVERTON - HISTORY AND ATTRACTIONS

• Historically a crossing point of the River Barle and a market town. Today it thrives on tourists who come here to visit surrounding Exmoor countryside and it's also a service centre for southern Exmoor. Compact and pretty with a good variety of shops. Its geographical position also meant a number of mills were established here. There is a pleasant walk along the old leat which once powered 6 mills. To the north-east of the church lie the remains of a 10 foot waterwheel which powered a smithy.

• **Guildhall Heritage Centre** Includes cottage showing living conditions in the 19th century and Exmoor Photographic Archive. Easter - Nov.

• **All Saints Church** Medieval tower. Nearby is the **Belfry Tree**, split by lightening in the 19th century. Banded together by a blacksmith it split again in a 1975 gale.

• The unusual **Town Hall** on Fore St. dates from the nineteenth century and has a double flight of external steps to the first floor.

• **The National Park** administrative headquarters is housed in a former workhouse that once accommodated up to 52 paupers. Information centre in library.

A group outing on Exmoor (section 5)

DULVERTON - ACCOMMODATION

Crispins Restaurant & Rooms, 26 High St (01398) 323397. Closed in Feb.
£££-other meals in restaurant-PL-DR-LAU-SEC. Dulverton centre.
Town Mills (01398) 323124. £££/£. In Dulverton town centre.
Springfield Farm, Ashwick Lane (01398) 323722. £££/£-PL-DR-SEC-WKSH.
Highercombe (01398) 323451 or 07000 700303. £££-£-PL-DR-LAU-SEC.

Also try: Lion Hotel (01398) 323444. Northcombe Farm Camping Barn (01398)
323118. 0.75 miles north of Dulverton.

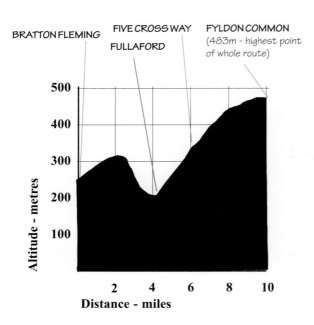

DULVERTON - OTHER INFORMATION

Tourist Information Exmoor National Park Visitor Centre. Part of library
building on Fore St (01398) 323841
Market Days Every third Friday in Town Hall.
Early Closing Thursday (applies only to chemist).
Banks Natwest (cashpoint), in front of church.
🚲 Enquire in local shops for possible help.

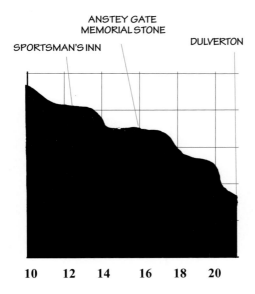

The rolling hills of Exmoor (section 5)

Near Moorgate Cross on Exmoor (section 5)

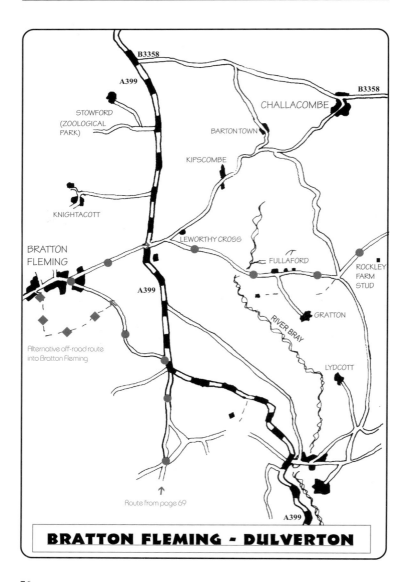

BRATTON FLEMING - DULVERTON

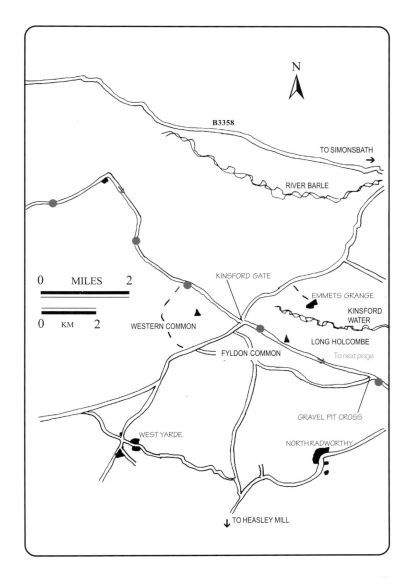

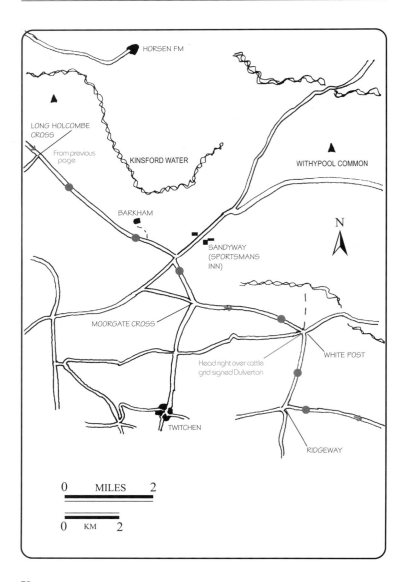

HORSEN FM

LONG HOLCOMBE CROSS

From previous page

KINSFORD WATER

WITHYPOOL COMMON

BARKHAM

SANDYWAY
(SPORTSMANS
INN)

N

MOORGATE CROSS

WHITE POST

Head right over cattle
grid signed Dulverton

TWITCHEN

RIDGEWAY

0   MILES   2

0   KM   2

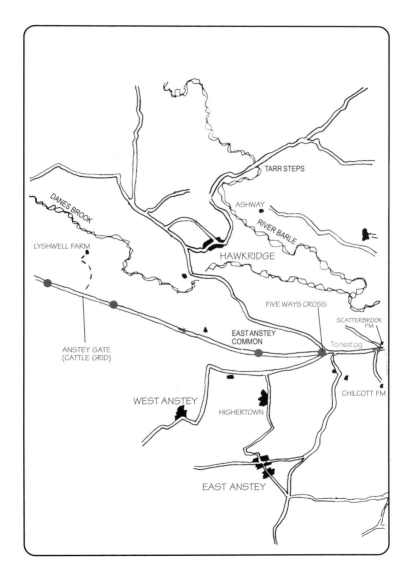

TARR STEPS

ASHWAY

DANES BROOK

RIVER BARLE

LYSHWELL FARM

HAWKRIDGE

FIVE WAYS CROSS

SCATTERBROOK FM

ANSTEY GATE
(CATTLE GRID)

EAST ANSTEY
COMMON

To next pg

WEST ANSTEY

CHILCOTT FM

HIGHERTOWN

EAST ANSTEY

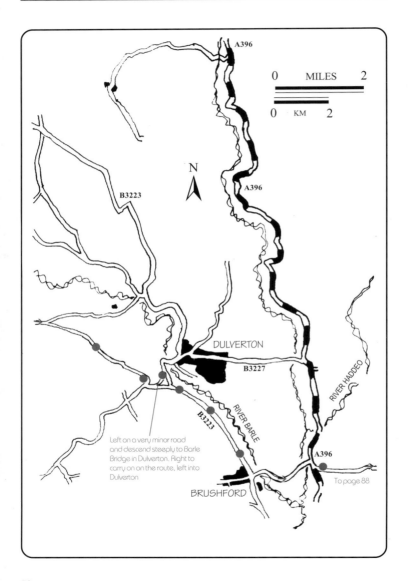

A396

0   MILES   2

0   KM   2

B3223

N

A396

DULVERTON

B3227

RIVER HADDEO

RIVER BARLE

B3223

Left on a very minor road and descend steeply to Barle Bridge in Dulverton. Right to carry on on the route, left into Dulverton

A396

To page 88

BRUSHFORD

WEST COUNTRY WAY LANDSCAPES

Above: Padstow harbour (section 1)
Below: Sunset over the River Parrett near Bridgwater (section 8)

Above: Near Glastonbury Tor (section 8)
Below: Exmoor ponies (section 5)

Above: View looking south-west, climbing the Mendips (section 8)
Below: Bampton village (section 6)   Overleaf: Market Place, Glastonbury (section 8)

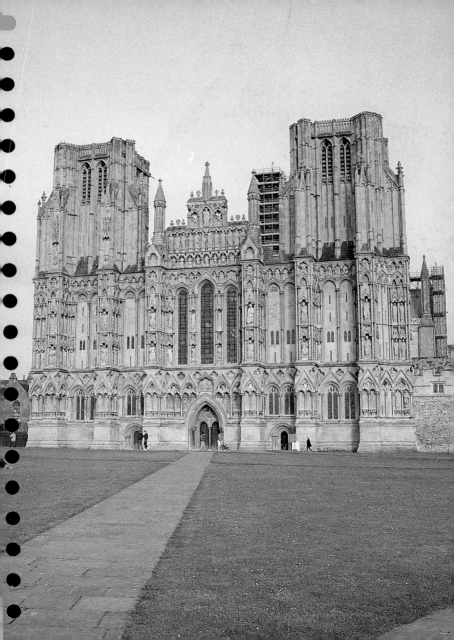

WEST COUNTRY WAY ARCHITECTURE

Above: Thatched cottage and village cross, Marhamchurch (section 2)
Below: Royal Crescent, Bath (section 9)   Previous page: Wells Cathedral (section 8)

TRAILS

Left: The Tarka Trail near Bideford
(section 4)

Below: Bristol - Bath Railpath
(section 9)

Previous page: Iron Bridge on the Camel
Trail (section 1)

6 DULVERTON - LANGFORD BUDVILLE

Section Distance 30 miles / 48 km   **Off-road** 9 miles / 16 km

Accumulated Distance 158.5 miles / 255 km

The Route Winding, undulating quiet country roads characterise the route from Dulverton to the charming town of Tiverton, passing the impressive Knightshayes Court on the way. Note that some sections of the Grand Western Canal tow-path may be much slower than anticipated if muddy. The last 6 miles or so use minor roads through the delightful villages of Greenham and Langford Budville.

DULVERTON TO TIVERTON

• **Bampton** Market town with Georgian houses. 14 / 15 th century church with 500 year old yew trees. Exmoor pony fair in October. Small Midland Bank on Brook St. Exe Valley railway linked the town to Tiverton and Dulverton but closed in 1963. Local quarrying has also disappeared but quarry remains can be seen as you leave the village, on the left. There are also remains of a castle or fortified house at the east end of Castle St. with fine views over rooftops. Small information centre in village centre. Look out for unusual memorial on west side of church to clerk's son!
• **Knightshayes Court** A grand 19th century mansion with flamboyant Gothic architecture surrounded by gloriously formal gardens, some of the best in Devon. The architect of the ornate facade was sacked partly for his over-extravagance! The grand interior has smoking and billiard rooms along with a boudoir. April - Oct. except Friday. (01884) 254665. Admission charge. Restaurant (lunches, tea/coffee).

DULVERTON TO TIVERTON - ACCOMMODATION

Higher Langridge Farm, Exebridge (01398) 323999. £££-Evening meal-PL-DR-LAU-SEC. 2 miles from Brushford.
Anchor Inn, Exebridge (01398) 323433. £££££. PL(24 hours notice)-DR-LAU-SEC. 1.25 miles from route. Also full range of meals and guest beers.
Lodfin Farm, Morebath (01398) 331400. Feb-Nov. £££/£-DR-SEC-WKSH. 1 mile.
Swan Hotel, Station Road, Bampton (01398) 331257. £££-PL-DR-LAU-SEC-WKSH. On route.
Bridge House Hotel, Bampton (01398) 331298. ££££-PL-LAU-SEC. Near route.
Manor Hill House, Bampton (01398) 332211. £££/£-DR-LAU-SEC. Meals 12-2.30 & 6.30-9.30. On route.
Landrake Farm, Chevithorne (01398) 331221. March-Nov. £££-Evening meals £4-£7-PL-DR-SEC-Basic tools. Also ▲ £5 with H&C water & toilet. On route.

81

TIVERTON - HISTORY AND ATTRACTIONS

• **Market town** surrounded by industry (including much textile activity). The wealth created by past industrial activity, especially wool, has left a rich and varied legacy of buildings including many almshouses, a factory school, Baptist chapel and cornmarket.
• **Tiverton Museum** A variety of displays about West Country history. Railway gallery and lace-making machinery. (01884) 256295 Feb - Dec. Admission charge.
• **Tiverton Castle** Built between the 12th and 14th centuries, former home of the Earls of Devon. Fell to the Parliamentarians during the Civil War. Seasonal opening details ring (01884) 253200
• The 17th century **Blundell's School** was built by a wool merchant. Now owned by the National Trust as a private property but visitors can enter the gateway to admire the building.
• **St. Peter's Church** has fine 16th century ship carvings in the south porch.
• The water bubbling up from **Coggan's Well** in Fore St. has been doing so since the middle ages.
• **Town Hall** Handsome Italianate building with illuminated clock.
• **The Great House of St. George** Jacobean mansion previously used by wool traders. Walled garden can be visited.

TIVERTON - ACCOMMODATION

Angel Guest House, 13 Peter St (01884) 251154. £££-PL-DR-SEC. 0.3 miles.
Bridge Guest House, 23 Angel Hill (01884) 252804. £££/£-PL-DR-LAU-SEC-WKSH. 0.3 miles.
Prince Regent Hotel, Lowmans Green (01884) 252882. £££££-PL-DR-LAU-SEC-WKSH. On the route.
Lodge Hill Guest House, Lodge Hill Farm (01884) 252907. £££/£-Dinner-PL-DR-LAU-SEC-WKSH.

Also try: Tiverton Hotel (01884) 256120. Hornhill (01884) 253352.

TIVERTON - OTHER INFORMATION

Tourist Information Phoenix Lane (01884) 255827
Market Days Pannier market, Tuesday to Friday
Early Closing Thursday
Hospital Tiverton District Hospital, William St. (01884) 253251
Banks Lloyds, Midland, Barclays and Natwest. All on Fore St. and all have cashpoints.
🚲 Maynards, 25 Gold St. (01884) 253979. Rons Cycle Centre, 10 Wellbrook St. (01884) 255750.

TIVERTON TO WELLINGTON

• The **Grand Western Canal** is now the basis of a country park used by walkers, anglers and a horse-drawn passenger boat. The route follows certain sections open to cyclists. Nineteenth century, it was designed by John Rennie, a pioneer of the canal age who was also responsible for many of London's bridges, despite the lack of any formal training! The overall canal scheme was originally supposed to link the Bristol and English Channels and avoid the hazards of rounding Cornwall. Attractive canal basin at Tiverton with lime kiln remains, tearooms and horse-drawn barge trips. After suffering from railway competition the canal became a country park in the 1970s.

• **Wellington** has historically been associated with serge cloth. Notable town hall and church. Not actually on the West Country Way at time of writing but there are plans to bring the route to the town. In any case you may wish to use the town's services such as B&Bs or its many shops. The **Wellington Memorial** is a monument to the famous Duke and was erected in the nineteenth century in Egyptian style on an outcrop of the Blackdown Hills and is visible from the route.

• **Globe Inn**, Sampford Peverell. Meals 12-2 & 6-10. Otter, Old Speckled Hen and Wadworth 6X ales.

• **Martlet Inn**, Langford Budville. Meals 12-2 & 7-9.30. Exmoor Ale and guest beer.

Grand Western Canal near Tiverton (section 6)

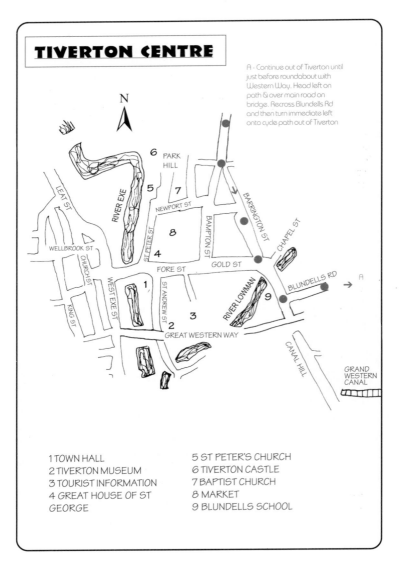

TIVERTON CENTRE

A - Continue out of Tiverton until just before roundabout with Western Way. Head left on path & over main road on bridge. Recross Blundells Rd and then turn immediate left onto cycle path out of Tiverton

N

PARK HILL

RIVER EXE

LEAT ST

NEWPORT ST

ST PETER ST

BAMPTON ST

BARRINGTON ST

CHAPEL ST

WELLBROOK ST

CHURCH ST

FORE ST

GOLD ST

BLUNDELLS RD

A →

WEST EXE ST

KING ST

ST ANDREW ST

RIVER LOWMAN

GREAT WESTERN WAY

CANAL HILL

GRAND WESTERN CANAL

1 TOWN HALL
2 TIVERTON MUSEUM
3 TOURIST INFORMATION
4 GREAT HOUSE OF ST GEORGE

5 ST PETER'S CHURCH
6 TIVERTON CASTLE
7 BAPTIST CHURCH
8 MARKET
9 BLUNDELLS SCHOOL

Rolling Devon countryside heading towards Knightshayes Court (section 6)

TIVERTON TO WELLINGTON - ACCOMMODATION

Challis, 12 Lower Town, Sampford Peverell (01884) 820620. £££-SEC-WKSH. Near route.
Boehill Farm, Sampford Peverell (01884) 820235. £££-DR-SEC-WKSH. Near Grand Western Canal.
Greenham Hall, Greenham Village (01823) 672603. £££/£-PL-DR-LAU-SEC. Near route.
Ridgeway Farm, Holcombe Rogus (On alternative route if canal towpath closed). (01823) 672644. £££. PL-DR-LAU-SEC-WKSH. ⚇ also.

Also try: Church Barn, Halberton (01884) 820358. Merrimeade Hotel, Sampford Peverell (01884) 821614. Gamlins Farmhouse, Greenham (01823) 672596. Orchard Haven, Langford Budville (01823) 672116. Easter - Oct.

⚇ **Gamlin Farm Caravan Park**, Greenham (01823) 672596. 28th March - Sept.
Minnows Caravan Park, nr Sampford Peverell, next to canal (01884) 821770. March - Jan.

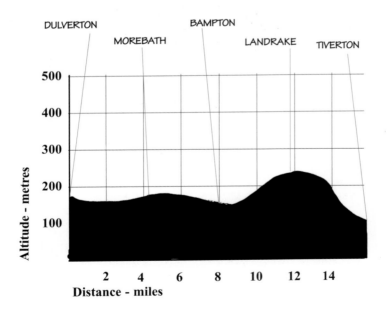

A quiet valley near Bampton (section 6)

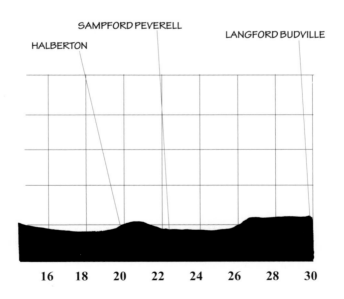

SAMPFORD PEVERELL

HALBERTON

LANGFORD BUDVILLE

16 18 20 22 24 26 28 30

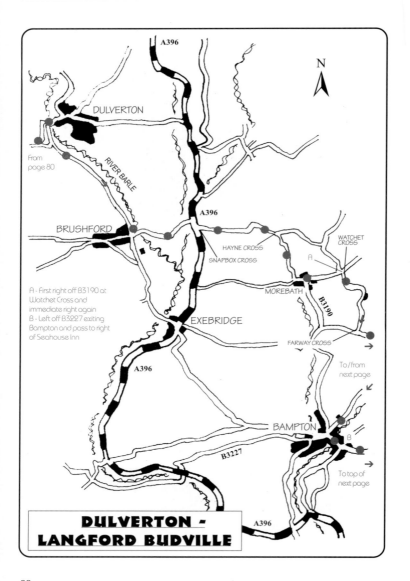

A396

N

DULVERTON

RIVER BARLE

From
page 80

A396

BRUSHFORD

HAYNE CROSS

SNAPBOX CROSS

WATCHET
CROSS

A

MOREBATH

B3190

A - First right off B3190 at
Watchet Cross and
immediate right again
B - Left off B3227 exiting
Bampton and pass to right
of Seahouse Inn

EXEBRIDGE

FARWAY CROSS

To/from
next page

A396

BAMPTON

B

B3227

To top of
next page

**DULVERTON -
LANGFORD BUDVILLE**

A396

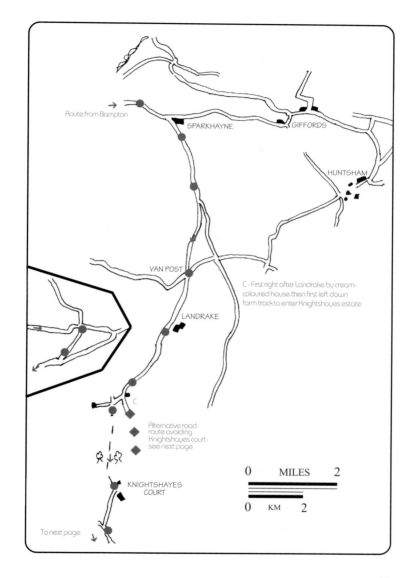

Route from Bampton

SPARKHAYNE

GIFFORDS

HUNTSHAM

VAN POST

C - First right after Landrake by cream-coloured house then first left down farm track to enter Knightshayes estate

LANDRAKE

C

Alternative road route avoiding Knightshayes court-see next page

0   MILES   2

0   KM   2

KNIGHTSHAYES COURT

To next page

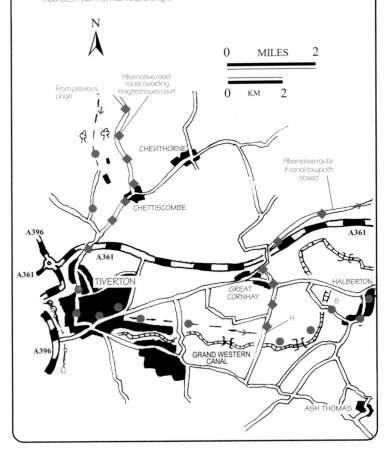

A - Path out of Tiverton finishes. Right on road to meet bridge and left before bridge onto canal towpath

B - After going over a brick aqueduct on the canal exit onto the road and right over the canal on the bridge. Come into Halberton at the end of Crown Hill. Left into Halberton then right up Church Path. Walk round church then right down Pond Hill to meet BUSY AND FAST main road and right.

N

0   MILES   2

0   KM   2

From previous page

Alternative road route avoiding Knightshayes court

CHEVITHORNE

Alternative route if canal towpath closed

CHETTISCOMBE

A396

A361

A361

A361

A396

TIVERTON

GREAT CORNHAY

HALBERTON

B

A

GRAND WESTERN CANAL

ASH THOMAS

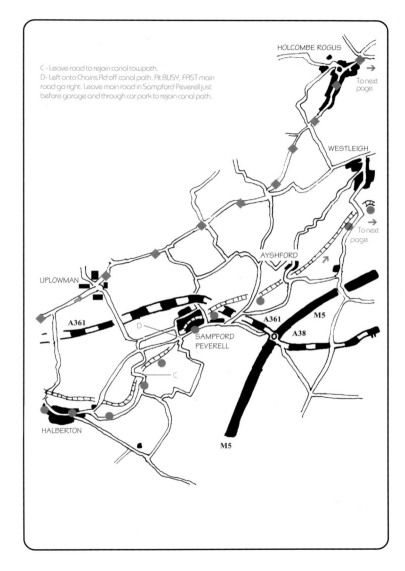

C - Leave road to rejoin canal towpath.
D - Left onto Chains Rd off canal path. At BUSY, FAST main road go right. Leave main road in Sampford Peverell just before garage and through car park to rejoin canal path.

HOLCOMBE ROGUS

To next page

WESTLEIGH

To next page

AYSHFORD

UPLOWMAN

A361

M5

A361

A38

SAMPFORD
PEVERELL

HALBERTON

M5

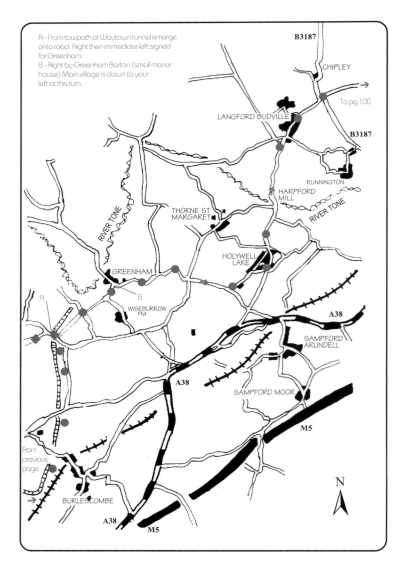

A - From towpath at Waytown tunnel emerge onto road. Right then immediate left signed for Greenham.
B - Right by Greenham Barton (small manor house) Main village is down to your left at this turn.

B3187

CHIPLEY

To pg 100

LANGFORD BUDVILLE

B3187

RUNNINGTON

HARPFORD MILL

RIVER TONE

THORNE ST MARGARET

RIVER TONE

HOLYWELL LAKE

RIVER TONE

GREENHAM

A

B

WISEBURROW FM

A38

SAMPFORD ARUNDELL

A38

SAMPFORD MOOR

M5

From previous page

N

BURLESCOMBE

A38

M5

7 LANGFORD BUDVILLE - BRIDGWATER

Section Distance 23.5 miles / 38 km   **Off-road** 10 miles / 16 km

Accumulated Distance 182 miles / 293 km

The Route One of the easiest sections of the whole route. A road descent into Taunton is followed by an extended ride on the excellently surfaced tow-path of the Bridgwater and Taunton Canal. Note there are two routes through Taunton town centre; one an off-road option that follows the River Tone and another which gives you the chance to see the town centre (the latter follows cycle lanes that run alongside busy town centre traffic).

WELLINGTON TO TAUNTON

Very quiet minor roads take you through a string of very small settlements. The largest and perhaps prettiest is Nynehead. You pass through the Vale of Taunton here, relatively flat compared to the surrounding Quantocks and Blackdown Hills.

TAUNTON - HISTORY AND ATTRACTIONS

• **County town**, fought over bitterly during the Civil War, during which most of the town was destroyed. Spread around the River Tone in the vale of Taunton Deane and surrounded by the Blackdown, Quantock and Brendon Hills.

• **Cider** is most traditionally associated with Taunton. Sheppy's Farm is 3 miles south-west of the centre where you can see traditional cider-making every autumn.

• **Norman castle**, essentially a 13th century Bishop's fortress, containing county and regimental museum. Great Hall was once Taunton's law court; 508 men were condemned to death here in Judge Jeffreys' 'Bloody Assize' following the 1685 rising by Monmouth. This protestant Duke had previously entered Taunton with 1,000 foot soldiers and by the time he reached Bridgwater he had 7,000 followers. He failed to take Bristol and his largely peasant army fell apart and he was executed. Open daily except Sun. Admission charge. There is a plaque near the High St. commemorating the ill-fated declaration of Monmouth as king in 1685.

• Nearby is the 14th century **Castle Bow**, the last remnants of the old town walls. The 13th century gateway near here was once the east gate of the castle.

• **Somerset Cricket Museum** Located in Priory Barn, dating from the 15th century. A wide collection of anything and everything connected with cricket. April-Nov. (01823) 275893. Admission charge.

• The route passes through **Goodland Gardens** by the River Tone. Sited on original town mills that made Taunton a famous 14th century wool town.

• Much other fine architecture includes the **Tudor House** on Fore St., the **Church of St Mary Magdalene**, the **Georgian architecture** of the High St. and 16th century **Municipal Buildings** in Corporation St.

TAUNTON - ACCOMMODATION

Hillview Guest House, Bishops Hull Road, Bishops Hull (01823) 275510. £££-PL-SEC-WKSH. On route.
Orchard House, Fons George, Middleway (01823) 351783. £££££-PL-SEC-WKSH. Near town centre.

Also try: Brookfield House (01823) 272786. Acorn Lodge (01823) 337613. Bryngwyn (01823) 254953. Southview (01823) 284639. Woodfields (01823) 337189. Old Inn, Bishop's Hull (01823) 284728

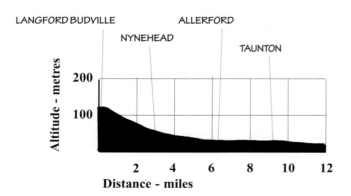

TAUNTON - OTHER INFORMATION

Tourist Information Paul St (Library Building) (01823) 336344
Market Days Tuesday (agricultural) and Saturday (agricultural & general)
Hospital Taunton and Somerset Hospital, Musgrove Park (01823) 333444
Banks North St. has a NatWest, Barclays and Midland, all with cashpoints.
🚲 Atkins Bike Shop (opposite cemetery at end of Mountway Rd), Bishops Hull.
The Bike Chain, Coal Orchard off St. James St. Ralph Colman Cycles, 79 Station
Rd. (01823) 275822. Bike Zone, Yarde Place (01823) 327006.

TAUNTON TO BRIDGWATER

• **Creech St Michael** 13th century church with fine wagon roof.
• The **Bridgwater and Taunton Canal** Opened in 1827 as part of the scheme to
link Bristol and Exeter which was never realised in full. Pillboxes alongside the
canal were built during WWII when many of the swing bridges were fixed in place.
The canal declined but was restored in the 1980s after years of lobbying. Coal
came from South Wales via the canal. Features the intriguing **Somerset Space
Walk** which starts at Maunsel Lock, where a large model of the sun explains how
model planets of our solar system radiate out from this point. They are shown on
plaques and to scale as you progress along the canal. One pace on this scale is
400,000 kms, Taunton to Bridgwater representing the full 'disc' of the solar system.
Maunsel Locks feature the last lock-keeper's cottage on the canal. Maunsel Canal
Centre has boat trips, tea-rooms and souvenirs. Easter-Sept.

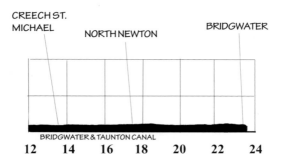

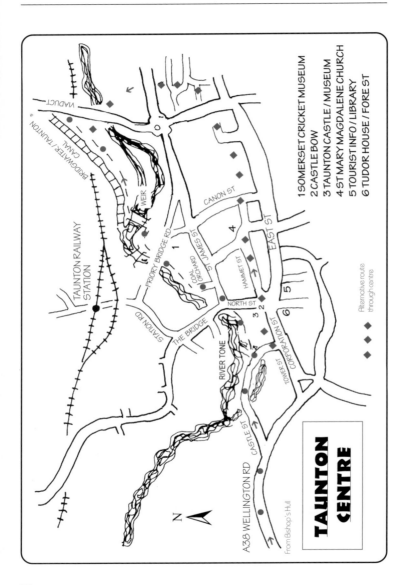

1 SOMERSET CRICKET MUSEUM
2 CASTLE BOW
3 TAUNTON CASTLE / MUSEUM
4 ST MARY MAGDALENE CHURCH
5 TOURIST INFO / LIBRARY
6 TUDOR HOUSE / FORE ST

TAUNTON CENTRE

Alternative route
through centre

VIADUCT
BRIDGWATER / TAUNTON CANAL
WEIR
TAUNTON RAILWAY STATION
PRIORY BRIDGE RD
STATION RD
THE BRIDGE
COAL ORCHARD
ST JAMES ST
CANON ST
HAMMET ST
EAST ST
NORTH ST
CORPORATION ST
TOWER ST
CASTLE ST
RIVER TONE
A38 WELLINGTON RD
From Bishop's Hull
N

TAUNTON TO BRIDGWATER - ACCOMMODATION

Creechbarn, Vicarage Lane, Creech St. Michael (01823) 443955. £££/£-PL (notice required)-DR-LAU-SEC-WKSH. Near route. Website http://www.netkonect.co.uk/h/humphreys/

BRIDGWATER - HISTORY AND ATTRACTIONS

• Once competed with Bristol as a **port town** hence abandoned quays, derelict landing stages, warehouses and Georgian houses (especially good houses on Castle St.). At low tide the **River Parrett**, which flows through the centre of town, reveals thick slabs of mud coating its sides, reminding you how near the northern coast of Somerset you are. Today it welcomes pleasure craft from the canal.

• Maritime and battle items on display in **Admiral Blake Museum**, Blake St. Detailed display on Battle of Sedgemoor where Monmouth, pretender to the throne was defeated. Features other local history and archaeology. Open all year. Free entry. (01278) 456127

• **Blake** is commemorated by a statue outside the market hall. An MP, he became an outstanding commander in Cromwell's Parliamentary Army.

• **Somerset Brick and Tile Museum** Features last surviving kiln at former works on East Quay. July and Sept 1998. Free admission.

• **Church of St Mary** 175 ft tower. The rebellious Duke of Monmouth surveyed the surrounding area from the tower before his defeat in 1685.

Bridgwater - Taunton Canal at Creech St. Michael (section 7)

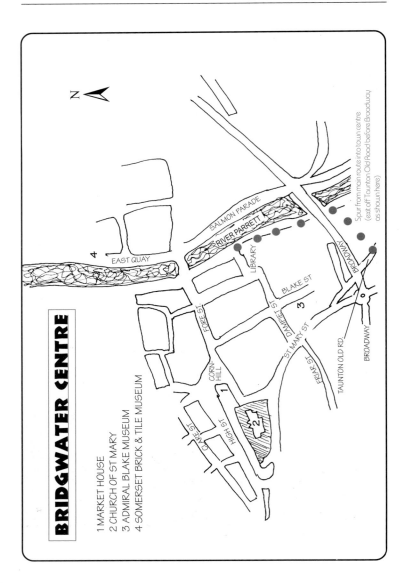

BRIDGWATER CENTRE

1 MARKET HOUSE
2 CHURCH OF ST MARY
3 ADMIRAL BLAKE MUSEUM
4 SOMERSET BRICK & TILE MUSEUM

Spur from main route into town centre
(exit off Taunton Old Road before Broadway
as shown here)

BRIDGWATER - ACCOMMODATION

Cokerhurst Farm, 87 Wembdon Hill (01278) 422330 Mobile (0850) 692065 ££££-PL-DR-LAU-SEC-WKSH. 1.5 miles.
Chinar, 17 Oakfield Rd (01278) 458639. From £££-DR-LAU-SEC.
Admiral's Rest Guest House, 5 Taunton Rd (01278) 458580. £££-PL-DR-SEC-WKSH. 0.25 miles from canal.
Brooklands Hotel, 56 North St. (01278) 423263. £££ and up. PL-DR-LAU-SEC.

Also try: Bower Green Pub (01278) 422926. Old Vicarage Hotel (01278) 458891. Woodlands (01278) 423442.

BRIDGWATER - OTHER INFORMATION

Tourist Information 50 High St. (01278) 427652. Open -Easter to autumn.
Market Days Cornhill Market, Monday - Saturday. Wednesday general and cattle market.
Early Closing Thursday
Hospital Bridgwater General, Salmon Parade (not 24 hrs). (01278) 451501
Banks Barclays, High St. NatWest, York Buildings. Midland, Fore St. Lloyds, Cornhill. All have cashpoints.
🚲 St. John Cycles, 91-93 St. John St. (01278) 441516. The Bike Chain, 101a Taunton Rd. (01278) 423640

By the River Parrett, Bridgwater centre (section 7)

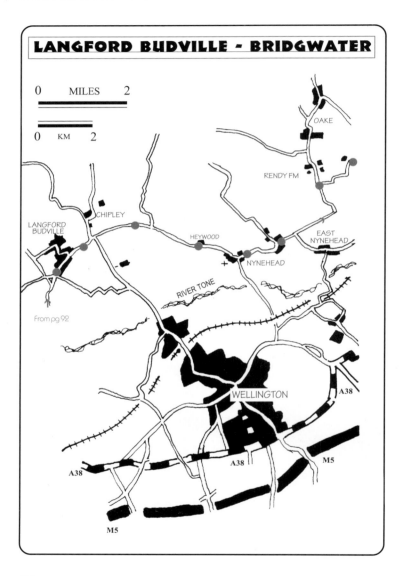

LANGFORD BUDVILLE - BRIDGWATER

0 MILES 2

0 KM 2

OAKE

RENDY FM

CHIPLEY

LANGFORD
BUDVILLE

HEYWOOD

EAST
NYNEHEAD

NYNEHEAD

RIVER TONE

From pg 92

WELLINGTON

A38

A38

A38

M5

M5

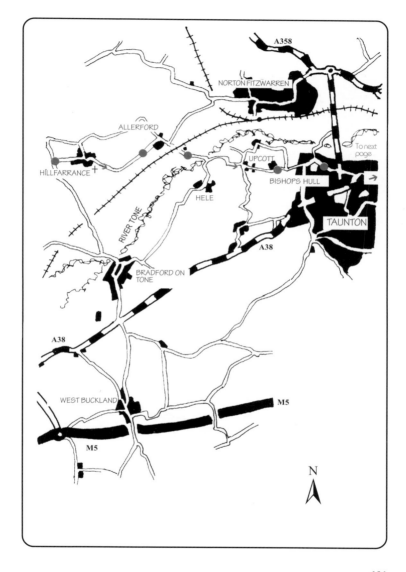

Idyllic property on the Taunton - Bridgwater Canal (section 7)

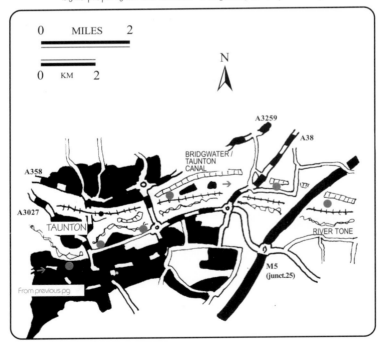

A - Shortly after passing under the A361 leave the towpath on a small swingbridge and follow the road parallel to the canal up to Maunsel Lock. Briefly rejoin the canal path here.
B - At Lower Maunsel Bridge leave the canal and follow the map into North Newton.

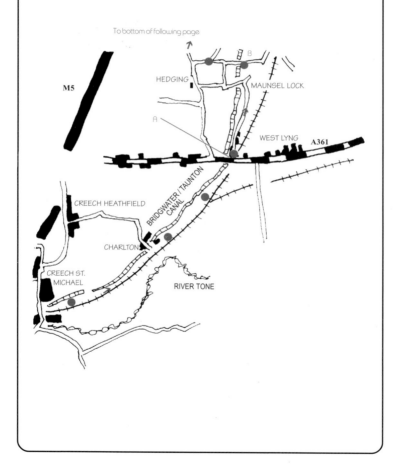

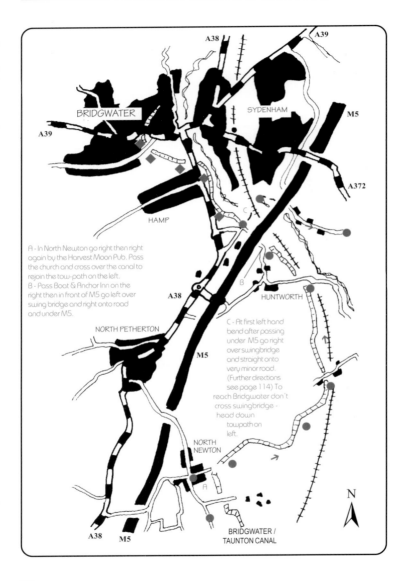

A38
A39
BRIDGWATER
SYDENHAM
M5
A39
A372
HAMP
C

A - In North Newton go right then right again by the Harvest Moon Pub. Pass the church and cross over the canal to rejoin the tow-path on the left.
B - Pass Boat & Anchor Inn on the right then in front of M5 go left over swing bridge and right onto road and under M5.

B
A38
HUNTWORTH

NORTH PETHERTON
M5

C - At first left hand bend after passing under M5 go right over swingbridge and straight onto very minor road. (Further directions see page 114) To reach Bridgwater don't cross swingbridge - head down towpath on left.

NORTH NEWTON
A
N

A38 M5
BRIDGWATER / TAUNTON CANAL

8 BRIDGWATER - PRIDDY

Section Distance 30 miles / 48 km   **Off-road** 3 miles

Accumulated Distance 212 miles / 341 km

The Route A flat, easy start gives way to the gentle folds of the Polden Hills; a new route, some of it off-road, is being negotiated and will bring more of the Polden villages onto the route. The flats of the Somerset Levels are best seen as you descend onto them after the Polden Hills; a rather surreal landscape of peat extraction workings and drainage ditches, backed by the dramatically rising Tor at Glastonbury, with its crowning medieval chapel. The only real blot on the landscape are the new light industrial and housing developments which mar what would be an otherwise classic approach to Glastonbury.

BRIDGWATER TO GLASTONBURY

• **Chedzoy** Small, quiet village on the **Somerset Levels**. Church typical of many in Somerset with its characteristic tower and numerous bench ends. Village name reflects the natural history of the Levels; being made up of a stream name and 'island' it reflects the time when this very flat area was surrounded by water and marsh, probably crossed by causeways linking island villages. 6,000 years ago the Sweet Track crossed the Levels and is thought to be Europe's oldest trackway. Monks at nearby Glastonbury encouraged land reclamation in medieval times and today the area is agricultural land criss-crossed by drainage ditches, known as rhynes and often bordered by pollarded willows. There are still pockets of special natural history interest where intensive agriculture has not undermined natural flora and fauna.

• **Kings Sedge Moor** is an area of partially drained former marsh, now a haven for wildlife, crossed by the route after leaving Bridgwater. Wading birds and wagtails are common, especially in autumn. The Kings Sedgemoor Drain is the main drainage ditch for the area. The Battle of Sedgemoor took place in this area in 1685 and was the last on English soil. For details see the section on Bridgwater 'History and Attractions'.

• **Ring O'Bells Pub**, Ashcott. Meals 12-3 & 7-10 (last orders). Moor Beer-Withy Cutter and guest ales. CAMRA Somerset Pub of Year 1998.

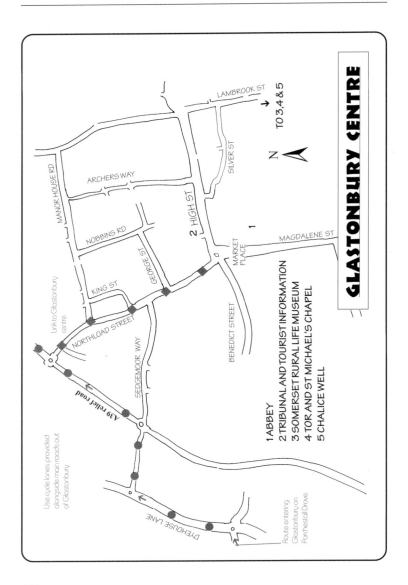

GLASTONBURY CENTRE

LAMBROOK ST

TO 3, 4 & 5

N

SILVER ST

MANOR HOUSE RD

ARCHERS WAY

2 HIGH ST

NOBBINS RD

MAGDALENE ST

GEORGE ST

MARKET PLACE

1

KING ST

BENEDICT STREET

Link to Glastonbury centre

NORTHLOAD STREET

SEDGEMOOR WAY

A39 relief road

DYEHOUSE LANE

Use cycle lanes provided alongside main roads out of Glastonbury

Route entering Glastonbury on Porchestall Drove

1 ABBEY
2 TRIBUNAL AND TOURIST INFORMATION
3 SOMERSET RURAL LIFE MUSEUM
4 TOR AND ST MICHAEL'S CHAPEL
5 CHALICE WELL

BRIDGWATER TO GLASTONBURY - ACCOMMODATION

1 Priory Cottages, Chilton Polden Hill (01278) 723054. March-Oct. £££. PL-LAU-SEC-WKSH. 1 mile off route.
Sunnyside, 34 Taunton Rd, Pedwell (01458) 210097. £££-PL-DR-LAU-SEC-WKSH. On route.

Also try: Honeysuckle, Catcott (01278) 722890.

⚠ **Fairways Touring Park**, Bawdrip (north of Chedzoy) (01278) 685569 1st March
- 15th Nov. **Bramble Hill Camping Park**, Walton (01458) 442548. About 1 mile
from route, south-east of Ashcott.

Vicars' Close, Wells - a superbly preserved medieval street (section 8)

GLASTONBURY - HISTORY AND ATTRACTIONS

• A **market town** on hills rising above the Somerset Levels. It is not difficult to see how Glastonbury gained a mystical reputation hundreds of years ago, as the hills would have risen up out of a sometimes flooded plain. Once supposedly known as Avalon in Celtic mythology - the Island of the Blessed Souls. Latterly it seems to have become a mecca for spiritualism, eastern mysticism and other modern-day alternative creeds (at least judging by the town centre shops), as well as being a market town and international tourist centre. If you want a dream-catcher this is the place to get it!

• The town is most strongly associated with its **abbey**. King Arthur and his Queen Guinevere are said to have been buried amongst the 13th century ruins here and it is supposedly the site where the Christianisation of England began with the planting of the Holy Grail (the cup used by Christ at the Last Supper). The destruction you see today is largely the result of Henry VIII's Dissolution of the Monasteries. Museum and display area give greater detail on the history. Entrance on Magdalene St. near Market Place. Open daily. (01458) 832267. Admission charge.

• **The Tribunal** in the High Street is where judges passed sentence in the name of the influential Abbots of Glastonbury. Dating from the fifteenth century. Now the information centre as well as housing the **Glastonbury Lake Village Museum.** Based on the finds of a 19th century archaeologist it shows how iron-age people lived on small islands surrounded by water and marshland, travelling between settlements by wooden canoes and walkways. Open daily. (01458) 832954

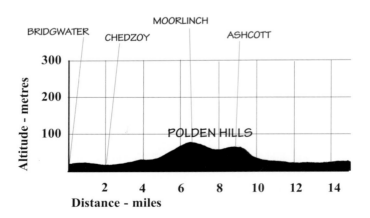

• **Chalice Well** A small garden has been built around this ancient spring, associated with druids and Joseph of Arimathea. The supply of drinkable water emerging from the ground comes from deep within the earth and has never been known to dry up. Chilkwell St. Entrance fee. (01458) 831154

• **Somerset Rural Life Museum** is housed in a 14th century tithe barn with an impressive collection of vintage farm machinery and other details of rural history. Open daily except winter Sundays. Admission charge & refreshments. (01458) 831197

• **St. Michael's Chapel** sits majestically on top of the hill of **Glastonbury Tor**. Affords a great view of the Levels. These 14th century remains are now roofless and empty. Half a mile's steep walk from the edge of Glastonbury centre.

GLASTONBURY - ACCOMMODATION

12-13 Norbins Rd (01458) 834606. £££-PL-DR-LAU-SEC-WKSH. 0.5 miles.
46a High St (01458) 832214. £££-DR-SEC. Town centre.
Melrose, 17 Bere Lane (01458) 832016. £££-DR-SEC. 10 minutes walk from centre.
King William Hotel, 19 Market Place (01458) 831473. ££££-PL-SEC. Town centre.
Glastonbury Backpackers, Crown Hotel, Market Place (01458) 833353. £/£-All meals available-PL(notice needed)-DR-SEC. Hostel accommodation. On route.

Also try: Pippin (01458) 834262. 46 Bove Town (01458) 833684.

⚠ **Isle of Avalon Touring Park**, on Godney road out of Glastonbury (01458) 831437.

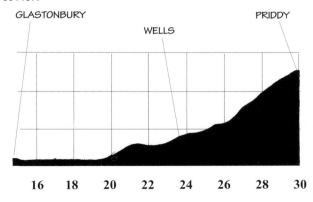

GLASTONBURY - OTHER INFORMATION

Tourist Information The Tribunal, 9 High St. (01458) 832949
Market Days Tuesday
Early Closing Wednesday
Banks Midlands, Lloyds, Barclays and NatWest are on the High St (latter two have no cashpoint). Barclays and NatWest have cashpoints near Safeways.
🚲 Pedlers, Magdalene St. (01458) 831117

WELLS - HISTORY AND ATTRACTIONS

• England's **smallest city**, with a medieval feel to it, known as the capital of the Mendips. A lot of fine architecture; Chapter House, Vicars' Close, Llewellyn's Almshouses, Old Deanery, Chain Gate and the Old Almshouses are a few examples.
• Most famous for its **cathedral** which has number of outstanding features such as West Front statuary, perhaps the greatest gallery of medieval sculpture in Europe, whilst inside jousting knights emerge from a beautiful astronomical clock every quarter hour (one of the oldest working clocks in the world). Huge 'scissor ' arches support the weight of the tower. Open daily with regular, free guided tours. Cloister restaurant.
• **Bishop's Palace** is one of England's oldest inhabited houses surrounded by defensive curtain wall and moat. On the surrounding moat swans ring the bell for food. Edward III gave permission for the heavy fortifications here. Spring waters keep the moat full and flow through the High St. These 'wells' gave the city its name. Reached through the 'Bishop's Eye' arch or cathedral cloisters. Easter - Oct. Open daily. Admission charge.
• **Vicars' Close** Oldest continuously inhabited, complete medieval street in Europe completed in the 14th century as a home for the College of the Vicars Choral. Through the arch on the northern side of the cathedral the close is accessible to the public.
• **Wells Museum** has findings from Wookey Hole including the skeleton of the 'Witch of Wookey' - a 1000 year old cave dweller. New display on building of the cathedral plus much more. Open daily in summer but closed Mon & Tues, Nov - Easter. (01749) 673477.

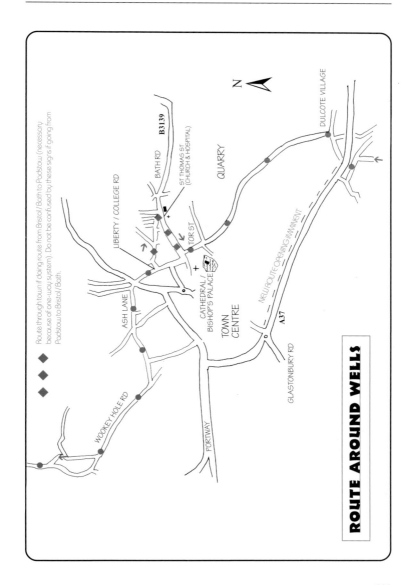

N

DULCOTE VILLAGE

B3139

BATH RD

LIBERTY / COLLEGE RD

ST THOMAS ST
(CHURCH & HOSPITAL)

QUARRY

TOR ST

ASH LANE

NEW ROUTE OPENING IMMINENT

A37

CATHEDRAL /
BISHOP'S PALACE

TOWN
CENTRE

GLASTONBURY RD

WOOKEY HOLE RD

PORTWAY

Route through town if doing route from Bristol / Bath to Padstow (necessary because of one-way system). Do not be confused by these signs if going from Padstow to Bristol / Bath.

ROUTE AROUND WELLS

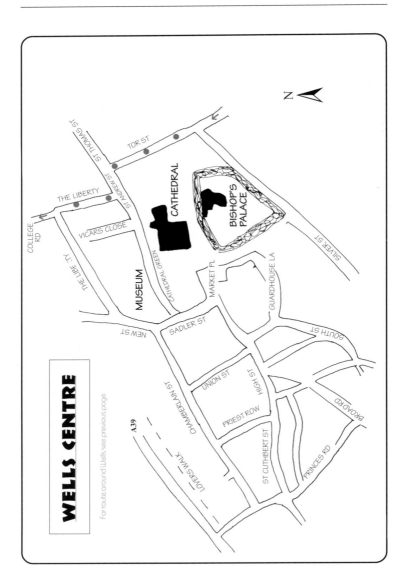

WELLS - ACCOMMODATION

Infield House, 36 Portway (01749) 670989. ££££-PL-DR-LAU-SEC-WKSH. 0.5 miles.
The Old Poor House, 7a St Andrew St. (01749) 675052 Mobile 0498-608517. £££-DR-LAU-SEC-WKSH. Near route.
The Limes, 29 Chamberlain St. (01749) 675716. £££/£-PL-DR-LAU-Basic tools. Near route.
The Crown at Wells, Market Place (01749) 673457. £££££-PL-LAU(not always possible)-SEC. Near route.
'Number Nine' 9 Chamberlain St. (01749) 672270. £££/£-PL-DR-LAU-SEC. Near route.

Also try: 30 Mary Road (01749) 674031. Milton House (01749) 672165.

⚠ **Birdwood House Camping**, Bath Road, Wells (1.5 miles north of centre). (01749) 679250.

WELLS - OTHER INFORMATION

Tourist Information Town Hall, Market Place (01749) 672552
Market Days Wednesdays & Saturdays. Market Square.
Early Closing Wednesday
Hospital Wells Health Centre, Glastonbury Rd. (01749) 672137
Banks Barclays, NatWest, Midland and Lloyds in the High St. (All with cashpoints)
🚲 Bikes & Bits, 31 Broad St. (01749) 670260. Trevor's Cycles, 49 Cuthbert St. (01749) 670868

WELLS TO PRIDDY

• **Wookey Hole Caves and Mill** Take a trip through the underground limestone chambers here and witness the fantastic rock formations. The mill here manufactures hand-made paper from cotton. The site is owned by Madame Tussaud's and includes a small waxworks exhibition and Victorian funfair exhibits. Open daily. Admission charge. (01749) 672243
• **Ebbor Gorge** Accessed from the first car park on the climb out of Wells. Waymarked walks around this fine example of a Mendip limestone valley.
• **Priddy** stands on top of a limestone plateau on the Mendip Hills. Famous for the historic burial mounds of Priddy Nine Barrows. A stack of hurdles (used for sheep pens) on the green is said to have stood there for 300 years, originally used for making sheep pens during the sheep fair. August 18th sees the traditional sheep fair. **New Inn** Meals 12-2 & 7-10. Bass, Wadworths 6X, Fullers London Pride.

WELLS TO PRIDDY - ACCOMMODATION

Milton Manor Farm, Old Bristol Rd, Upper Milton ((01749) 673394. £££-DR-LAU-SEC-WKSH. 1 mile from Wookey Hole.
New Inn, Priddy (01749) 676465. £££-PL-DR-SEC. On route.

Also try: Ganymede, Wookey Hole (01749) 677250. Pink Lodge, Wookey Hole (01749) 677384. Miners Arms, Priddy (01749) 870217.

Λ **Homestead Park**, Wookey Hole (01749) 673022. **Ebborlands**, Wookey Hole (01749) 672550. **Mendip Heights**, Priddy (01749) 870241. 1st March - 15th Nov.

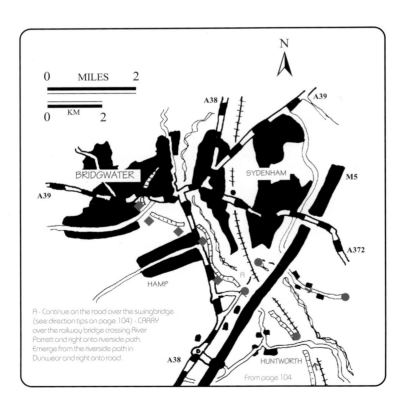

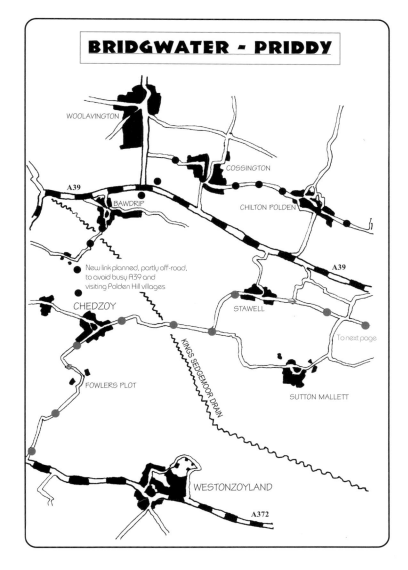

BRIDGWATER - PRIDDY

WOOLAVINGTON

COSSINGTON

A39

BAWDRIP

CHILTON POLDEN

A39

New link planned, partly off-road, to avoid busy A39 and visiting Polden Hill villages

CHEDZOY

STAWELL

To next page

FOWLERS PLOT

KINGS SEDGEMOOR DRAIN

SUTTON MALLETT

WESTONZOYLAND

A372

115

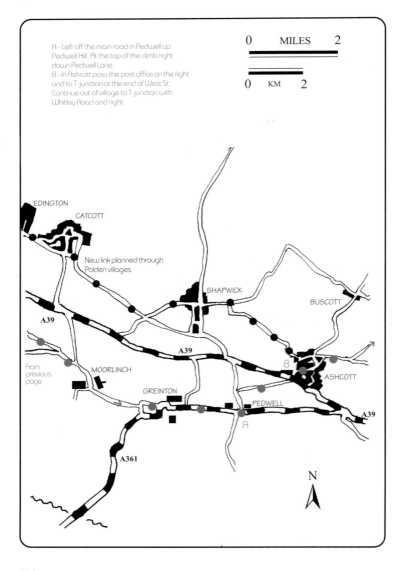

A - Left off the main road in Pedwell up Pedwell Hill. At the top of the climb right down Pedwell Lane.
B - In Ashcott pass the post office on the right and to T-junction at the end of West St. Continue out of village to T-junction with Whitley Road and right.

0   MILES   2

0   KM   2

EDINGTON

CATCOTT

New link planned through Polden villages

SHAPWICK

BUSCOTT

A39

A39

From previous page

MOORLINCH

B

ASHCOTT

GREINTON

PEDWELL

A

A39

A361

N

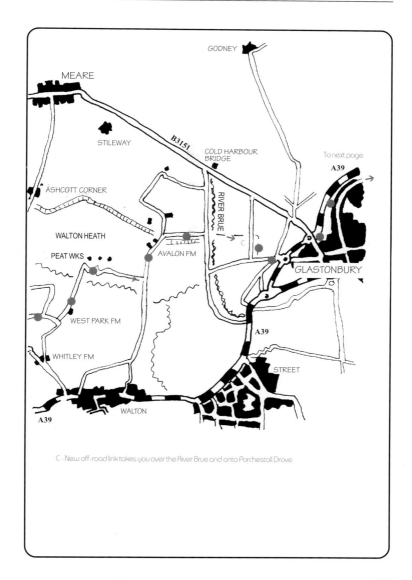

GODNEY

MEARE

STILEWAY

B3151

COLD HARBOUR BRIDGE

To next page

A39

ASHCOTT CORNER

RIVER BRUE

WALTON HEATH

PEAT WKS

AVALON FM

C

GLASTONBURY

WEST PARK FM

A39

WHITLEY FM

STREET

A39   WALTON

C - New off-road link takes you over the River Brue and onto Porchestall Drove

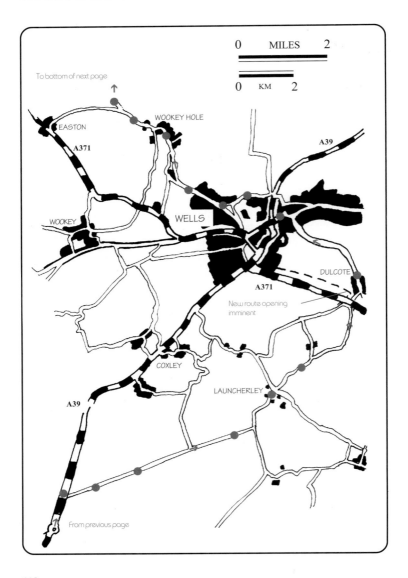

Typical Levels scenery of rhynes (ditches) and pollarded willows - nice and flat!
(section 8)

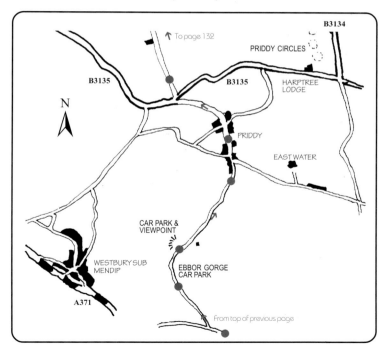

9 PRIDDY - BRISTOL / BATH

Section Distance Bristol 35.5 miles / 57 km   **Off-road** 10 miles / 18km
Bath 28.5 miles / 46 km   **Off-road** 7.5 miles / 12km

Accumulated Distance Bristol 247.5 miles / 399 km
Bath 240.5 miles / 395 km

The Route

The final leg is a relatively easy one; largely descending after crossing the flat top of the Mendips with only a couple of small stiff climbs, to reach the virtually flat Bristol to Bath railway path at Saltford. From here you must decide whether to finish in the classical elegance of Bath or in the cosmopolitan variety of Bristol, impressively sited on the Avon, around the Floating Harbour area. If you've still got the legs and the time you could visit both. Saltford - Bath is around 5 miles / 8km and Saltford-Bristol around 12 miles / 19 km. Both are impressive ends to the route; in Bath by Bath Spa station and in Bristol by the imposing Cathedral.

PRIDDY TO BRISTOL / BATH RAILWAY PATH

• **Chew Valley Lake** is in fact a reservoir supplying water to Bristol. Birdwatchers should look out for grebes, kingfishers, woodpeckers and little owls. Information centre, free admission & refreshments. Hides available.
• **Bristol to Bath Railway Path** The northern Bristol option is longer but has more diversions including several sculptures and Bitton station on the **Avon Valley Railway.** Holiday outings run on this steam and diesel section of track south into the Avon Valley and north to Oldland Common. Details from (0117) 9327296. The sculptures along the trail were part of Sustrans' pioneering efforts on the path. Lots of commuter use gives this section a different feel to much of the rest of the route. The whole route was constructed in stages from 1979 - 86.

PRIDDY TO SALTFORD - ACCOMMODATION

Try: Warren Farm, Charterhouse (01761) 462674. **Centaur**, Bishop Sutton (01275) 332321. Valley Farm, Stanton Drew (01275) 332723. Orchard House, Chew Stoke (01275) 333143. Woodbarn Farm, Chew Magna (01275) 332599. Greenacres, Stanton Wick (01761) 490397. Prospect Villa, Saltford (01225) 873211.

🚲 Bits-Z-Cars, High St. Staple Hill, Bristol (0117) 9566868. Park Cycles, 84 Broad St. Staple Hill, Bristol (0117) 9754310.

Looking back to the south-west after climbing the Mendips (section 8)

BATH - HISTORY AND ATTRACTIONS

• Bath is hugely popular with visitors. This spa town's long and interesting history has left it with an **architectural legacy** that makes it a byword for classical elegance. A real treasure trove of history; you will need several days to see everything! Bath is particularly associated with John Wood (one of its main architects) and Beau Nash (who popularised it as the height of fashion); both really put Bath on the map in the eighteenth century. Spring waters would cure your ills and you could attend numerous social occasions such as fashionable dances!

• **Roman Baths and Museum** The baths are arguably the greatest Roman remains in Britain. Known as Aquae Sulis (waters of Sul - a local Celtic God) they were based around a hot spring whose waters had supposed health benefits. Romans later added 'Minerva' to the title - their own god of healing. Main attraction is the original pool, Great Bath, 70ft long and 30ft wide, lined with the original lead and fed from a hot spring by the original Roman plumbing, producing 500,000 gallons of water daily. King's Bath is nearby as is the Roman Museum which contains fascinating coins, carvings and jewels. Open daily. Admission charge. (01225) 477785

• **The Abbey** An imposing Gothic style building. Modern stained glass combines well with the rest of the structure which dates from the 15th century. In the south aisle is a tablet to Beau Nash who helped popularise Bath as a spa town in the 18th century. Donation requested. (01225) 422462. **The Abbey Vaults** History of worship and archaeology on the site. Admission charge (01225) 422462

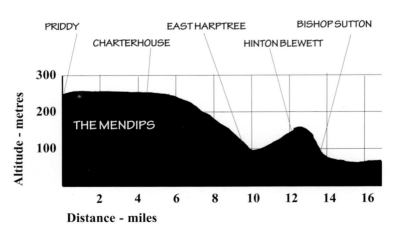

• **The Circus** is one of the most photographed areas of Bath with its three arcs, each of 33 houses, surrounding a large open space. Built in the 18th century. Look out for plaques on various houses telling which famous figure once lived there. Nearby is the **Royal Crescent**, the world's first crescent, and like the Circus built by John Wood. Lined with 114 Ionic columns. No. 1 has been restored in period style and opened to the public and is accordingly a World Heritage Site. March - Oct. Sun. pm. Admission charge. (01225) 428126

• **Pulteney Bridge** Another classic architectural view of Bath based on the medieval Ponte Vecchio in Florence, though designed by Robert Adam in 1771. Lined with shops on either side of the roadway it beautifully spans the Avon. Best seen from the River Avon towpath.

• **Great Pulteney Street** A long range of classical buildings, none later than the 18th century.

• The **Assembly Rooms** were the most expensive construction in Bath at the time of building at a cost of £20,000. Erected in the 18th century for polite society breakfasts, fancy dress balls and card games. Destroyed by fire in 1942 but later restored. Also houses the Museum of Costume. Open daily. Admission charge to museum.

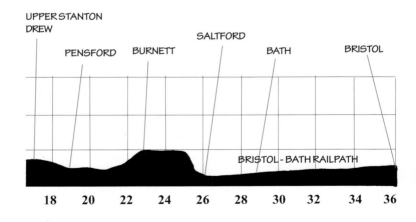

UPPER STANTON
DREW

PENSFORD   BURNETT

SALTFORD

BATH   BRISTOL

BRISTOL - BATH RAILPATH

18   20   22   24   26   28   30   32   34   36

• **Pump Room** This beautiful 18th century room covers the hot waters of the King's Bath. Statue of Beau Nash. Open daily. Free entry.

• **Building of Bath Museum** Including the history of Bath stone from which the city was built. Opening varied seasonally. The Paragon (01225) 333895

• **Bath Industrial Heritage Centre** Based around remaining artifacts of a family business where nothing was ever thrown away! Includes reconstructions of local crafts. Julian Rd. (01225) 318348

• **Holburne Museum** At the end of Great Pulteney Street this former hotel has collections of silver, porcelain, glass, furniture and paintings by such artists as Stubbs and Gainsborough. Surrounded by the gorgeous Sydney Gardens, crossed by a Chinese style bridge. Varied seasonal opening. Admission charge. (01225) 420465

• **Museum of English Naive Art** Unique museum has collection of paintings depicting everyday life plus collections of inn signs and weather vanes.

• Also look out for: **Bath Postal Museum** 8 Broad St (01225) 460333 **Cross Bath** At the end of Bath St hot springs emerge **East Gate** is the only surviving medieval gateway into the city **Herschel House and Museum** The personal house of the private astronomer of George III. 19 New King St. (01225) 311342 **Market** 12-sided domed and glazed interior **Book Museum** Bookbinding and Bath in literature. Manvers St. (01225) 466000 **Queen Square** Great 18th century architectural project **RPS National Centre of Photography** History of photography and contemporary exhibitions from major photographers. Milsom St. (01225) 462841 **Sally Lunn's House** Bath's oldest house with small museum and tea-rooms 4 North Parade Passage (01225) 461634 **Saracen's Head** City's most ancient inn on Broad St **Victoria Art Gallery and Museum** Paintings, prints, ceramics and glass plus topographical views of old Bath (01225) 477772 **The Guildhall** has magnificent Adam-style interiors. Restricted opening (01225) 477724 **Museum of East Asian Art** 12 Bennett St (01225) 464640 **American Museum & Gardens** American life from the 17th to the 19th centuries. Room reconstructions and many artifacts. Signed from Bathwick Hill (01225) 460503

BATH - ACCOMMODATION

Fairhaven Guest House, 21 Newbridge Rd (01225) 314694. £££-DR-SEC. Approx 1 mile from station.

Wellsgate, 131 Wells Rd. (01225) 310688. ££££/£-SEC-Some tools. 0.6 miles from centre.

The White Guest House (01225) 426075. £££££-PL-SEC. 0.5 miles from centre.

Bath Youth Hostel, Bathwick Hill (01225) 465674. £-DR-LAU-SEC. YHA members only. 0.8 miles from Bath Spa station.

Also try: Marisha's (01225) 446881. Aran House (01225) 317977. Ashgrove (01225) 421911. Astor House (01225) 429134. Arney Guest House (01225) 310020.

⚠ **Newton Mill Camping**, Newton Road, Bath (01225) 333909.

BATH - OTHER INFORMATION

Tourist Information Abbey Chambers, Abbey Church Yard (01225) 477101
Market Days Monday - Saturday, Guildhall general market.
Hospital Royal United Hospital, Combe Park (01225) 428331
Banks Various branches around the city but the main high street banks all have branches with cashpoints on Milsom St.
🚲 Avon Valley Cyclery, Arch 37, rear of Bath Spa Station (01225) 446267. John Bikes Ltd, 80-84 Walcot St. (01225) 334633. City Cycles, 6 Monmouth Place, (01225) 311595.

Pulteney Bridge over the Avon, Bath (section 9)

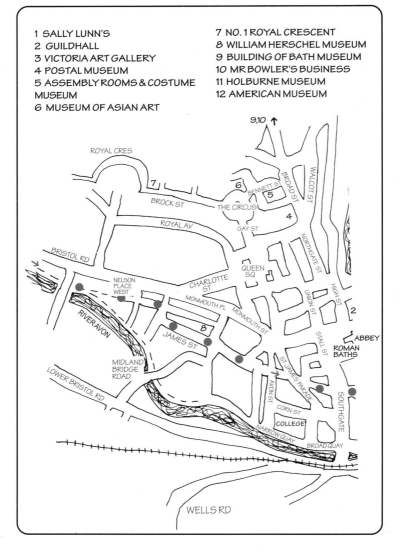

1 SALLY LUNN'S
2 GUILDHALL
3 VICTORIA ART GALLERY
4 POSTAL MUSEUM
5 ASSEMBLY ROOMS & COSTUME MUSEUM
6 MUSEUM OF ASIAN ART
7 NO. 1 ROYAL CRESCENT
8 WILLIAM HERSCHEL MUSEUM
9 BUILDING OF BATH MUSEUM
10 MR BOWLER'S BUSINESS
11 HOLBURNE MUSEUM
12 AMERICAN MUSEUM

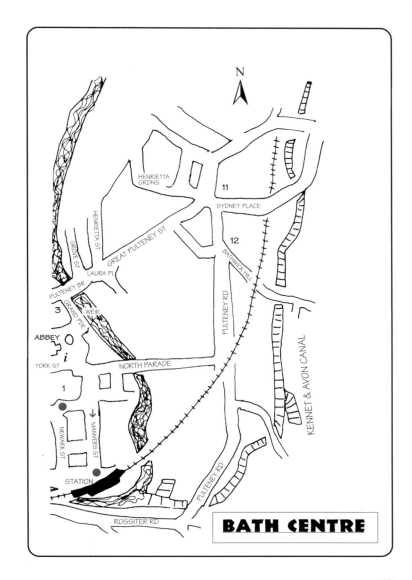

BATH CENTRE

BRISTOL - HISTORY AND ATTRACTIONS

• Although a little way from the coast, spread out behind the **Avon Gorge**, Bristol was once England's **busiest port** and one of the greatest in the whole world. Much of its maritime wealth was built on the **slave trade** as the city saw the exchange of black slaves for rum, sugar and tobacco brought from the West Indies. This trade declined after the American War of Independence and the abolition of slavery in 1833. Despite dock improvements by Isambard Kingdom Brunel, Bristol lost a lot of trade to Liverpool, which, unlike Bristol, was not a tidal port. The expense of dock charges meant the world's first transatlantic steamer, the *Great Western*, was forced to operate from Liverpool and not Bristol, where it was built.

• The **Floating Harbour** is at the heart of the city. Restored, it has not been used since the 1970s. *SS Great Britain* is in her original dry dock on the south side. Designed by Brunel, she was the first ocean-going ship to be built of iron and is being restored to her former glory. Admission charge. (0117) 9291843. Harbour boat trips leave from near the *SS Great Britain*. Look out for the statue of Neptune at the head of the western arm of the Floating Harbour. Other harbourside attractions include the following: The **Arnolfini Gallery** displaying modern art and with a popular cafe. The **Maritime Heritage Centre** is next to the *SS Great Britain*. (0117) 9260680. The **Watershed**, a collection of former transit buildings, now houses an arts complex (0117) 9276444, shops and bars. **Welsh Back** is a quay area full of old warehouses, including the brick-built 1871 Granary in a style known as 'Bristol Byzantine'. **Bristol Industrial Museum** Port of Bristol gallery and dockside exhibits. Princes Wharf. Admission charge. (0117) 9251470

• **Corn St.** still houses the 18th century **Corn Exchange** and outside are the bronze tables known as **nails**, where bargains were once struck for 'cash on the nail'.

Bristol - Bath Railpath (section 9)

• **King St.** contains a lot of fine architecture. **Llandoger Trow** is a half-timbered building once the haunt of smugglers and pirates. This inn, built in the 17th century, takes its name from a Welsh coastal vessel that once frequented Bristol. The **Theatre Royal** is Britain's oldest working theatre.

• **Broad St.** is a well preserved narrow street! It includes the **Council House** (1827), the **Grand Hotel** with its Renaissance style facade and a plaque marking the site of **High Cross**, the centre of the medieval town. There are also many fine buildings around the 17th century **Christmas Steps**.

• **St. Nicholas' Market** was reconstructed in 1850 and is still used as a market.

• The **Edward Everard Building** is a superb example of Art Noveau with its richly coloured marble-ware tiles. Other fine constructions include the Bristol branch of the **Bank of England** and the **Foster's Almshouses**, next to the **Chapel of the Three Kings of Cologne**. Another outstanding bank is Lloyds, built in Venetian style with a superb frieze.

• Bristol is also a city of churches. **St. Mary Redcliffe** is a graceful medieval building with a 285 ft spire whilst the smaller **Wesley's Chapel**, on the Horsefair, is the oldest Methodist chapel in the world. Much of the **Cathedral** is Norman including chapter house, gatehouse, the walls of the south transept and the east walk of the cloister. Route finishes outside this fine building. The **Lord Mayor's Chapel** has Flemish stained glass and Spanish tiles.

• The **City Museum and Art Gallery** has local archaeological and geographical relics plus a replica of the Bristol Boxkite biplane and a fine art collection. Admission charge. (0117) 9223571. Also look out for the **Exploratory**, a 'hands-on' science centre, near Temple Meads station, (0117) 9079000, and **Harveys Wine Museum** 12 Denmark St. (0117) 9275036.

• Several old houses include **Red Lodge** with fine oak panelled room, Park Row, (0117) 9211360, **Chatterton House**, birthplace of the eponymous poet and the **Georgian House** with 18th century furniture and fittings. 7 Great George St. (0117) 9211362

• The **Clifton area** of the city, with its fine 18th century buildings, allows you stunning views over the Avon Gorge and **Clifton Suspension Bridge.** Yet another feature of the city designed by Brunel, it was opened 5 years after his death in 1864, following delays due to financial problems. Its 700ft plus span hangs magically 245 ft above the Avon. On the Clifton side is an **observatory** (0117) 9741242, and beneath this a passage leads to **Giant's Cave** which opens onto a ledge above the spectacular limestone gorge.

• **Cabot Tower** Remembers the 15th century Venetian navigator who discovered Newfoundland with the aid of Bristol merchants. His journey from Bristol across the Atlantic took 35 days. The 150 ft structure is on Brandon Hill. Nearby is **Jacob's Well**, first recorded in 1042, with oldest known Hebrew inscriptions in Britain. Another local landmark is **University Tower**, built by the tobacco magnate Wills Sons as a memorial to their father. An outstanding 215ft neo-Gothic construction.

• **Temple Meads Station** has its original gothic facade.

BRISTOL - ACCOMMODATION

Arches Hotel, 132 Cotham Brow (0117) 9247398. ££££/£-DR-SEC-WKSH. 0.75 miles from city centre.
 Bristol International Youth Hostel, 14 Narrow Quay (0117) 9221659. £-LAU-SEC. 0.6 miles from Temple meads station.

Also try: Basca House (0117) 9422182. Gala Guest House (0117) 9653938. Harpenden (0117) 9240016. 8 Southernhay Avenue (0117) 9832927. Sunderland Guest House (0117) 9737249. The Hawthorns (July - Sept - University accommodation) (0117) 9238366.

⚠ **Baltic Wharf Caravan Club Site**, Bristol City Centre (0117) 9268030.

BRISTOL - OTHER INFORMATION

Tourist Information St Nicholas Church, St Nicholas St. (0117) 9221557
Market Days Monday to Saturday, St. Nicholas Market.
Hospital Bristol Royal Infirmary, Marlborough St. (0117) 9230000
Banks Various branches around the city, but all the main high street banks have branches and cashpoints on Corn St.
🚲 Mud Dock Cycleworks, 40 The Grove (0117) 9292151. Palmers Cycles, 11-13 Stokes Croft. (0117) 9249550.

Roman statue on Bristol - Bath Railpath (section 9)

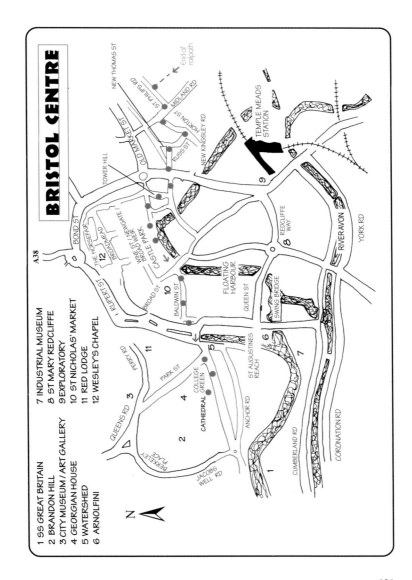

BRISTOL CENTRE

A38

1 SS GREAT BRITAIN
2 BRANDON HILL
3 CITY MUSEUM / ART GALLERY
4 GEORGIAN HOUSE
5 WATERSHED
6 ARNOLFINI
7 INDUSTRIAL MUSEUM
8 ST MARY REDCLIFFE
9 EXPLORATORY
10 ST NICHOLAS' MARKET
11 RED LODGE
12 WESLEY'S CHAPEL

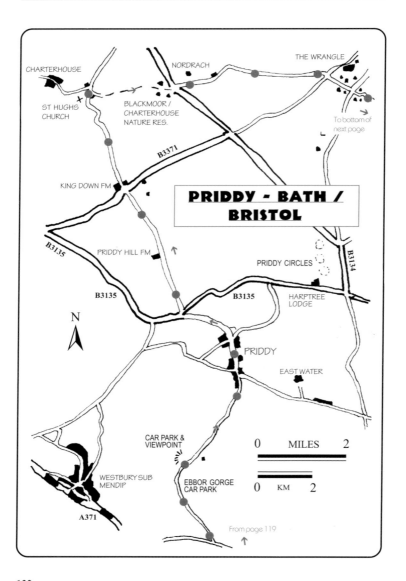

CHARTERHOUSE

ST HUGHS
CHURCH

NORDRACH

THE WRANGLE

BLACKMOOR /
CHARTERHOUSE
NATURE RES.

To bottom of
next page

B3371

KING DOWN FM

PRIDDY - BATH / BRISTOL

B3135

PRIDDY HILL FM

PRIDDY CIRCLES

B3134

B3135

B3135

HARPTREE
LODGE

N

PRIDDY

EAST WATER

CAR PARK &
VIEWPOINT

0   MILES   2

WESTBURY SUB
MENDIP

EBBOR GORGE
CAR PARK

0   KM   2

A371

From page 119

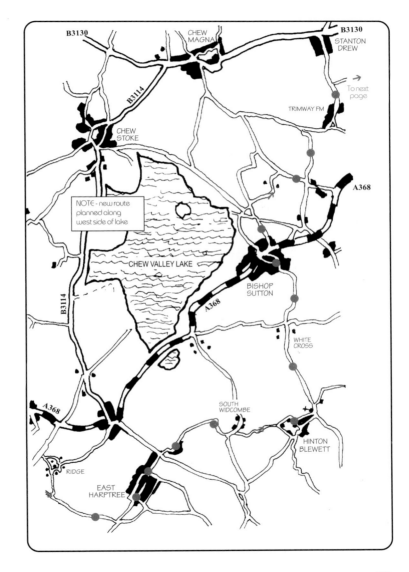

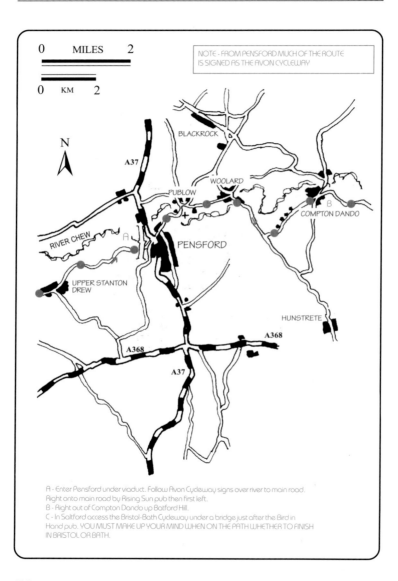

0   MILES   2

0   KM   2

NOTE - FROM PENSFORD MUCH OF THE ROUTE IS SIGNED AS THE AVON CYCLEWAY

N

A37

BLACKROCK

WOOLARD

PUBLOW

B
COMPTON DANDO

RIVER CHEW

A

PENSFORD

UPPER STANTON DREW

HUNSTRETE

A368

A368

A37

A - Enter Pensford under viaduct. Follow Avon Cycleway signs over river to main road. Right onto main road by Rising Sun pub then first left.
B - Right out of Compton Dando up Batford Hill.
C - In Saltford access the Bristol-Bath Cycleway under a bridge just after the Bird in Hand pub. YOU MUST MAKE UP YOUR MIND WHEN ON THE PATH WHETHER TO FINISH IN BRISTOL OR BATH.

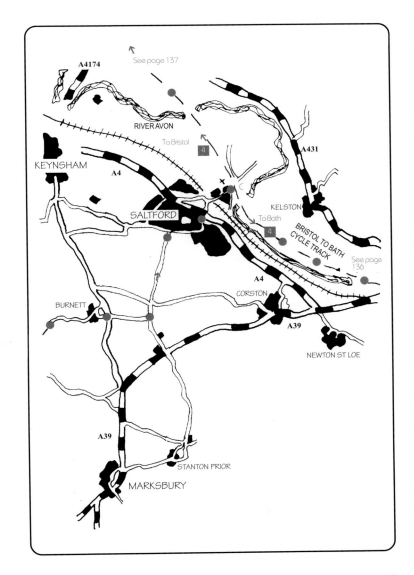

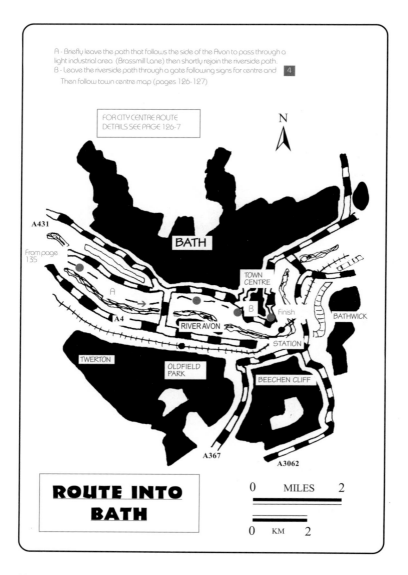

A - Briefly leave the path that follows the side of the Avon to pass through a light industrial area (Brassmill Lane) then shortly rejoin the riverside path.
B - Leave the riverside path through a gate following signs for centre and 4

Then follow town centre map (pages 126-127)

FOR CITY CENTRE ROUTE
DETAILS SEE PAGE 126-7

N

A431

BATH

From page
135

A

A4

TOWN
CENTRE

B

Finish

BATHWICK

RIVER AVON

STATION

TWERTON

OLDFIELD
PARK

BEECHEN CLIFF

A367

A3062

ROUTE INTO BATH

0   MILES   2

0   KM   2

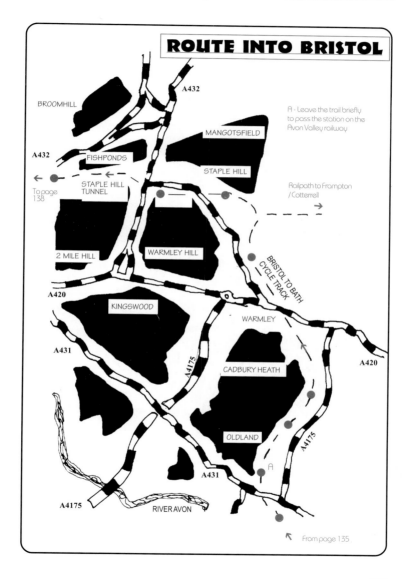

ROUTE INTO BRISTOL

A432

BROOMHILL

A432

FISHPONDS

MANGOTSFIELD

STAPLE HILL

A - Leave the trail briefly to pass the station on the Avon Valley railway

To page 138

STAPLE HILL TUNNEL

Railpath to Frampton / Cotterell

2 MILE HILL

WARMLEY HILL

BRISTOL TO BATH CYCLE TRACK

A420

KINGSWOOD

WARMLEY

A431

A4175

CADBURY HEATH

A420

OLDLAND

A4175

A431

A

A4175

RIVER AVON

From page 135

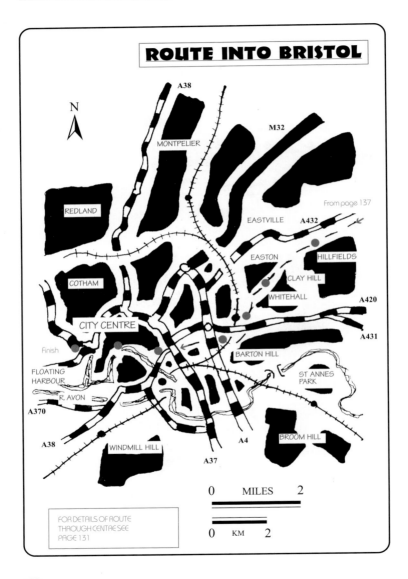

ROUTE INTO BRISTOL

N

A38

M32

MONTPELIER

REDLAND

From page 137

EASTVILLE   A432

EASTON   HILLFIELDS

COTHAM   CLAY HILL

WHITEHALL   A420

CITY CENTRE   A431

Finish   BARTON HILL

FLOATING
HARBOUR   ST ANNES
PARK

R. AVON

A370

A38   BROOM HILL

WINDMILL HILL   A4

A37

0   MILES   2

0   KM   2

FOR DETAILS OF ROUTE
THROUGH CENTRE SEE
PAGE 131

INDEX

CITIES, TOWNS, VILLAGES & PLACES IN MAIN TEXT

Entries in red type indicate town maps

ACCOMMODATION / CAMPING INDEX

Λ at the end of an accommodation section indicates camping site.

ABOUT THE AUTHOR

Richard Peace is a freelance author and photographer. He was educated at Queen Elizabeth Grammar School, Wakefield and Magdalen College, Oxford. After several periods of foreign travel he qualified as a solicitor and began outdoor writing as a hobby during his time in a solicitor's office. He has ten titles to his name. He has also written for several national outdoor magazines.

OTHER BOOKS BY RICHARD PEACE

All guides are illustrated with either drawings or black and white photos and come complete with sketch maps and lots of other practical information.

CYCLING GUIDES

THE ULTIMATE C2C GUIDE £6.95 ISBN 1-901464-02-4
Excellent Books
Simply the most popular long distance cycling route in the UK, completed by thousands each year. From the Cumbrian coast to Newcastle or Sunderland the route crosses the Lake District and Northern Pennines. Includes maps, accommodation, direction tips, background and full colour photos.

YORKSHIRE DALES CYCLE WAY £5.50 ISBN 1-870141-28-8
Hillside Publications
An outstanding 130 mile route circling the entire national park and beginning in the market town of Skipton. Malham, Settle, Ingleton, Dent, Hawes and Swaledale precede a superb return down Wharfedale to Grassington. Minor roads follow leafy dale bottoms then rise over majestic moorland tops.

WEST YORKSHIRE CYCLE WAY £4.99 ISBN 1-870141-38-5
Hillside Publications
This 152 mile route starts in Haworth and takes in many of the contrasts of West Yorkshire, from pastoral plains to rolling Pennine scenery. Visit Otley Chevin, Pontefract Castle, Aberford and the Worth and Holme Valleys.

MOUNTAIN BIKING WEST AND SOUTH YORKSHIRE £5.99
ISBN 1-870141-40-7 Hillside Publications
20 rides between 8.5 and 16.5 miles from the high Pennines to the rolling eastern plains. Includes Ilkley Moor, Calderdale, Holme Valley and the Barnsley Canal.

BIKING COUNTRY GLASGOW, CLYDE VALLEY AND LOCH LOMOND £5.99
ISBN 1-870141-45-8 Hillside Publications
18 well-researched and attractive routes exploring the hidden corners around
Glasgow. Using canal tow-paths, special cycle tracks, farm tracks and minor roads
the routes range from 6 to 18 miles.

MOUNTAIN BIKE LANCASHIRE AND SOUTH PENNINES £5.99
ISBN 1-901464-00-8 Excellent Books
20 off-road routes, visiting numerous scenic highlights in the Red Rose county and
South Pennines. 6.5 to 20 miles to suit all levels of mountain biker. Includes famed
scenery such as the Bowland Fells and Pendle Witch Country.

LEISURE RIDES IN THE PEAK DISTRICT AND DERBYSHIRE £5.95
ISBN 1-901464-01-6 Excellent Books
25 trails and circular routes throughout the Peak District and Derbyshire. Ideal for
families and occasional / leisure riders. Many moderate length outings with longer
linear outings allowing you to do as much or as little as you like. Practical advice on
cycling with children plus cycle hire and eating details. Routes cover the Dark and
the White Peak areas and visitor attractions such as Chatsworth.

WALKING AND GENERAL GUIDES

YORK WALKS £2.50 ISBN 1-870141-47-4 Hillside Publications
5 classic walks around the city of York exploring the major tourist sites and many
lesser known features. Each theme walk traces an aspect of York's development
over the centuries. Also includes children's attractions and historic inns.

THE MACLEHOSE TRAIL AND ITS SURROUNDINGS £7.99
ISBN 962-7335-14-2 The Alternative Press, Hong Kong
Written during the author's period in Hong Kong teaching English, this is a complete
practical guide to the superb 100 kilometre walking trail that crosses the mountainous
New Territories of Hong Kong. A superb blend of cityscape and wild countryside
add up to a once- in-a-lifetime experience.

LANCASHIRE CURIOSITIES £6.95
ISBN 1-874336-42-3 The Dovecote Press
The latest in the line of the Dovecote Press's popular look at follies, buildings and
all things curious on a county by county basis. 80 interesting sites county wide,
profusely illustrated with quality black and white photographs.

*THE ABOVE BOOKS MAY BE OBTAINED AT ALL GOOD BOOK SHOPS OR
DIRECT FROM EXCELLENT BOOKS (DETAILS AT FRONT OF BOOK).*

CALLING ALL CYCLISTS !

Do you have any constructive comments or updates to information on the West Country Way route or this guide? As a dedicated and responsible publishing company we want to keep our guides as useful and bang up-to-date as possible, as we recognise that, over time, some changes may occur to route details. New editions are frequently updated and as guides are not bound until distribution to bookshops the latest information can be included in an addendum. Send in your comments and/ or information updates on the route and we will send a free guide of your choice to authors of the best letters (unfortunately not every letter will get a guide). You can also keep up to date with the latest releases from Excellent Books by requesting our free catalogue. All communications should be sent to:

Excellent Books
94 Bradford Road
Wakefield
West Yorkshire
WF1 2AE
Tel / Fax: 01924 - 315147

WANT TO KNOW MORE ABOUT SUSTRANS?

Full details of other Sustrans routes and a catalogue of their route maps, other products and subscription details are available by dialling their public information line on (0117) 9290888.